BACKGAMMON
FOR
SERIOUS
PLAYERS

Bill Robertie

CARDOZA PUBLISHING

FIRST EDITION

Copyright @ 1997 by Bill Robertie
- All Rights Reserved -

Libray of Congress Catalog No: 96-85062
ISBN: 0-940685-68-X

ABOUT THE AUTHOR

Bill Robertie is the world's best backgammon player and the only two-time winner of the Monte Carlo World Championships. In addition to this book, Robertie is the author of five other books on winning at backgammon and the co-publisher of Inside Backgammon, the world's foremost backgammon magazine. He's also is a chess master, winner of the U.S. Speed Chess Championship, and the author of five chess books.

His club and tournament winnings have allowed him to travel the world in style. Robertie currently makes his home in Arlington, Massachusetts.

BACKGAMMON AND CHESS BOOKS BY BILL ROBERTIE
Backgammon for Winners
Backgammon for Serious Players
Advanced Backgammon Volume 1: Positional Play
Advanced Backgammon Volume 2: Technical Play
Lee Genud vs. Joe Dwek
Reno 1986
Beginning Chess Play
Winning Chess Tactics
Winning Chess Openings
Master Checkmate Strategy

TABLE OF CONTENTS

1

INTRODUCTION

Winning at backgammon requires mastering two phases of the game: **dynamic checker play**, using your checkers as weapons to pin your opponent in awkward positions; and **aggressive cube action**, using the doubling cube to maximize your wins in good positions and minimize your losses in bad positions.

Both parts of the game are essential. Without sharp checker play, you won't create the sorts of positions where you can outmaneuver and outplay your opponents. Without skillful use of the doubling cube, you won't earn as much from your good positions as you should. If you're going to be a big winner, you've got to master both parts of the game.

In this book, we'll show you the secrets of aggressive checker and cube play as practiced by the greatest masters of the game. You'll learn how to make your checkers work in multiple ways, how to build primes quickly when you need them, and how to drop back into holding positions and back games for more winning chances late in the game. You'll also learn the master's secrets for offering timely doubles, and how to decide whether a cube is a take or a drop.

By the time you've finished this book, you'll be starting to incorporate these ideas in your own games. The results will be impressive. Your checker play will put extra pressure on your opponents forcing them into cramped, awkward positions.

Your cubes will come at just the right moment, forcing tough decisions. And your improved technique will let you bring your games to winning conclusions, avoiding the upsets and turn-arounds that will plague your opponents.

Let's get started!

2

HOW TO USE THIS BOOK

The best way to study backgammon is by looking at actual games of good players. There you'll find, not contrived situations, but the sort of difficult yet fascinating positions that occur when backgammon is played by competitors who really understand the game. In this book I've collected five of the most interesting games from master play in the last few years. Each of the players is a first-class pro playing at the top of his game.

My first book, *Backgammon for Winners*, gave you a solid foundation for mastering the basic strategies of the game. In the games I've picked for this book, you're going to be introduced to a higher level of play, full of new ideas that we haven't encountered before. Read carefully; there's probably a lot here that you haven't seen before. By the time you've worked your way through the whole book, your understanding and your play will have advanced several levels.

Backgammon is best studied *actively*, not passively. It's easy to fall into the trap of reading through a book quickly, noting what the author has to say, telling yourself "Oh yes, that's pretty obvious" and moving on. Since backgammon moves are all just sitting there, waiting to be found, it's tempting to think that you would surely have found all these moves had you been sitting at the table.

I recommend a more active approach to reading this book.

Treat each game like a quiz, especially on your first pass. Try using a piece of paper or cardboard to cover a player's roll and move. Then move the paper to uncover just the dice roll, and ask yourself, "What would I play here?" If you want, write down your play on a separate piece of paper. Now expose the actual play and compare it to what you would have done.

By reading in this way, you'll compile a list of the plays you would have made differently. Now the explanations will be more meaningful, since you've already done the work of grappling with the problem yourself. At the same time, you'll want to read closely the comments on the plays you made correctly, since the comments may bring out some features of the position you hadn't considered.

3

BACKGAMMON TOURNAMENTS

Backgammon tournaments are held all over the world and throughout the year. On any given weekend, there will be local tournaments across the United States and throughout Europe. The game is currently catching on in South America, and many new clubs and events are starting there.

The biggest tournaments are frequent enough to comprise an informal tour, and a handful of professional players make the circuit. The big events start with Istanbul in January, then the Bahamas Pro-Am in February, followed by the Swiss tournament in Gstaad and St. Moritz in March. Then it's on to St. Tropez and Las Vegas in April and May, Venice in June, and The World Championship in Monte Carlo in July. A brief stopover in Cannes, then the highlight of the tour, the World Cup itself in Dallas. In October it's off to South America and the tournaments in Sao Paulo, Rio, and Buenos Aires, finishing up with the Las Vegas Open in November.

Tournaments are great places to meet new players, take a look at new boards and equipment, and pick up news of clubs opening. Most top tournaments have a lecture series for beginners and intermediates, while pros are always available for private lessons. Beginners shouldn't be intimidated, as every tournament has sections and activities designed especially for newcomers. And if you absorb the lessons in this book, you won't stay a beginner for long!

Backgammon Tournaments

Backgammon tournaments are run somewhat like tennis tournaments, using an elimination format. In the first round, players are paired at random. If the number of players is not equal to a power of 2 (16, 32, 64, 128, and so forth), some players will receive a bye, a free pass to the next round. Each round, half the players are eliminated, until only two players remain. These two players compete in the finals for the title of champion.

Eliminated players are dropped into a new event, called the *Consolation*. Losers in the Consolation are dropped into a final event, the last chance. Matches in the Consolation and Last Chance are typically shorter than in the main event.

In a typical tournament, about 60% of the prize money is allocated to the main event, with 30% in the Consolation and 10% in the Last Chance. Of course, the exact percentages and prizes are up to the tournament organizer. In addition to the main tournament with its Consolation and Last Chance, there are usually many jackpots and side events going on at the same time. Some players have been known to play over 100 matches during the course of a week-long competition.

A large tournament may take 7-9 days to complete. Smaller regional events might be held over a long weekend. A purely local event can be completed in a single day. Matches in regional and local events are much shorter than in the big international competitions.

Special Rules For Tournament Play

Tournament play is structured around matches which are played to a specified number of points. By tradition, the number of points in a match is always odd. In a local tournament, for example, the matches might start at 9 points, increasing as rounds are played to a 15-point final match. The longer the match, the more skill is involved in the outcome.

As in money play, the doubling cube is used. Players play games and add the points won in each game to their total score. When one player reaches the desired total, the match is over and he is the winner.

In tournament play, you don't have to double to win a gammon. That's different from money play, where in most clubs the doubling cube must be turned for a gammon or backgammon to be scored (the Jacoby rule).

Toward the end of a match, the Crawford Rule comes into play. Invented many years ago by John Crawford, the Crawford rule states that when a player's score reaches one point from victory, his opponent cannot double in the very next game. If the match continues beyond the next game, the cube can be used normally.

For example, Smith and Jones are playing a 9-point match, and Smith wins a game to make the score: Smith 8, Jones 4. The next game is the Crawford Game, and Jones cannot double in this game. (Smith, of course, has no reason to double.) Let's say Jones wins one point in the Crawford Game to make the score 8 to 5. In the following game, normal rules are back in effect and Jones can double as soon as he wishes.

Disputes between the players are settled by calling the tournament director, who will make a ruling. In certain exceptional cases, a panel of experienced players may be convened to make a ruling.

The Major Tournaments
Like golf and tennis, backgammon has a few events whose importance dwarfs the other tournaments. Here's a brief rundown of the biggest and most prestigious tournaments in modern backgammon.

The World Cup

The most important tournament in backgammon is the World Cup, held every other year in August in Dallas. What separates the World Cup from all other events is the extreme length of its matches. Each round in the main event is a best three out of five, 11-point series. In the consolation, matches start at 25 points (longer than the finals at most tournaments) and increase to a 29-point final. Chess clocks are used to time each match and ensure reasonably speedy play (and add a little extra pressure, besides). The World Cup is the most difficult tournament in backgammon to win, and in fact, no one but a top world-class pro has ever won the event. Here's a list of the winners, runners-up, and consolation winners of this grueling event.

FIRST PLACE	SECOND PLACE	CONSOLATION
1988: Joe Sylvester	Ray Glaeser	Bill Robertie
1990: Billy Horan	Tino Lechich	Yamin Yamin
1992: Mike Svobodny	Hal Heinrich	Malcolm Davis
1994: Billy Horan	Joe Sylvester	Hugh Sconyers
1996: Malcolm Davis	Kit Woolsey	Paul Magriel

The World Championship

The World Championship of Backgammon is held every July at Loew's Hotel in Monte Carlo. The event normally attracts about 400 players. Most participants are from Europe, although each year about 30 Americans make the journey. Matches in the main event begin at 17 points and increase to a 25-point final. With the shorter matches, the luck factor is much greater than in the World Cup, but the contest itself is always fascinating. Here are the winners of the last 20 World Championships:

20 WORLD CHAMPIONSHIPS

1977:   Richard Goodwin (USA)
1978:   Paul Magriel (USA)
1979:   Luigi Villa (Italy)
1980:   Walter Coratella (Mexico)
1981:   Lee Genud (USA)
1982:   Jacques Michel (Switzerland)
1983:   Bill Robertie (USA)
1984:   Mike Svobodny (USA)
1985:   Charles Sabet (Italy)
1986:   Clement Palacci (Italy)
1987:   Bill Robertie (USA)
1988:   Philip Marmorstein (Germany)
1989:   Joe Russell (USA)
1990:   Hal Heinrich (Canada)
1991:   Michael Meyburg (Germany)
1992:   Ion Ressu (Rumania)
1993:   Peter Thomsen (Denmark)
1994:   Frank Frigo (USA)
1995:   David Ben-Zion (Israel)
1996:   David Nehmad (Israel)

Istanbul

The Middle East holds the world's largest collection of backgammon players, but until quite recently no international tournaments were held in that area. The situation changed in 1992 when Israeli promoter and player Abraham Eitan began organizing a series of events at the Conrad Istanbul hotel. The event has quickly grown to be the most popular tournament in the world, with over 400 competitors at the 1996 event. It's held the third week of January every year.

	FIRST PLACE	RUNNER-UP
1992:	Thomas Lumper	Herve Pietraru
1993:	Gordon Cross	Paul Magriel
1994:	Bill Robertie	Stuart Hosen
1996:*	Peter Heitmuller	Matthias Korner

*1996 marked the first year that the tournament was moved from a December to a January format. (No year was actually skipped.)

The Bahamas Pro-Am Doubles

The Bahamas has been the scene of top-flight backgammon events ever since the very first international tournament was organized there by Prince Alexis Obolensky in 1964. That tournament grew into the Obolensky Cup, held during the 1960s and 1970s, but eventually discontinued in 1974.

The World Championship was held on Paradise Island until 1978, when it moved to Monte Carlo. For about ten years after that, a regular tournament on the international circuit was held every year in January, until the idea of a high-class doubles tournament caught on.

The idea of a Pro-Am doubles tournament was the brainchild of Lewis Deyong, a backgammon promoter from London. The format is a doubles tournament of 16 teams, each with a top tour professional paired with an enthusiastic amateur. The event takes place the first week of February at the Ocean Club on Paradise Island in the Bahamas. Here's a list of the winners:

1989:	Kent Goulding & Mo Sussman
1990:	Dennis Carlston & Jim Scott
1991:	Billy Horan & Katie Wright
1992:	Bill Ellis & Joel Silverman
1993:	Bill Robertie & Bill Bartholomay
1994:	Paul Magriel & Chico Brown
1995:	Paul Magriel & Steve Zolotow
1996:	Jim Colen & Joe Thomas

4

Backgammon games are recorded using a method called **backgammon notation**. It's easy to learn, and it lets us replay a backgammon game whenever we want to. Let's see how it works.

Diagram 1 shows the starting position of a backgammon game:

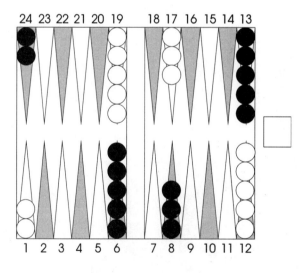

Notice that we've numbered all the points on the board, starting with point number 1 in the lower left and going all the way to point number 24 in the upper left. Using these point numbers, we can describe all the moves of a backgammon game.

In Diagram 1, Black is moving **clockwise**. His pieces move from the upper left quadrant to the right across the top half of the board, then to the left along the lower half ending up in the quadrant on the lower left. Black's pieces always move from higher numbered points to lower numbered points.

White's pieces move in the opposite direction, **counter-clockwise**. White's pieces end up in the upper left quadrant.

Suppose Black won the opening roll with a 31 (Black rolled a 3 and White rolled a 1, so Black would move first), and wanted to make his 5-point. In backgammon notation, we would write

1. Black 31: 8/5 6/5
This says: On the first roll of the game, Black rolled 31, and moved a piece from the 8-point to the 5-point, and another piece from the 6-point to the 5-point. The resulting position would look like this:

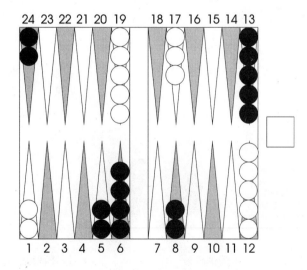

Now suppose that White rolled a 63, and elected to run with one of his two checkers on the 1-point. We'd write

2. White 63: 1/10
and the position would now look like this:

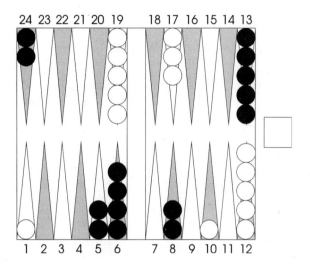

If you've understood this so far, congratulations! You've mastered backgammon notation.

There are a couple of more shorthand notations that you'll see throughout the book. Here they are:

Rolling doubles. When a player rolls doubles and moves his checkers in pairs, the move looks like this:

3. White 11: 19/20(2) 17/18(2)
This means White moved two checkers from the 19-point to the 20-point, and two more from the 18-point to the 17-point.

Hitting a blot. When someone hits a blot, we use the symbol *, like this:

4. Black 63: 24/15*
This means Black moved a checker from the 24-point to the 15-point, hitting a blot and sending it to the bar.

Bearing off. We indicate that checkers were borne off with the notation /off. For instance:

24. Black 65: 6/off 5/off

This means Black rolled a 65 and bore off two checkers.

That's all there is to it! When you play through the games, compare the position on your board at home with the diagrams in the book. WIthin a very short time you'll be reading the notation flawlessly.

5

GAME 1
BLACK: BILLY HORAN
WHITE: MATTHIAS PAUEN

Billy Horan has been recognized as one of the very top players in the world for some time. He's the only player to win the World Cup twice, in 1990 and 1994. He's also won the Athens tournament in 1994 and the Bahamas Pro-Am in 1991.

Matthias Pauen is one of the strongest German players. His best result so far has been second place is the Torrequebrada tournament in Spain in 1992.

Our first game was played in the semifinals of the great Athens tournament of 1994. Billy Horan of New York, the eventual winner of the event, met Matthias Pauen of Germany. The match was to 23 points. We're going to look at Game 5 of the match; at this point Pauen leads Horan 4 to 3.

1. Black 62: 24/18 13/11.
This is the modern way of playing an opening 6-2. With the 6, Black moves out to the opposing bar point (the 18-point), hoping that one of two things will happen: White will fail to hit this blot and Black will roll another 6 and **anchor** on the bar point next turn, or White will hit the blot but leave a blot of his own, and a return hit by Black will gain a lot of ground in the race. With the 2, Black puts a **builder** on the 11-point, which can be useful in the future in making the 5-point, 7-point, or 9-point.

Black had several other ways of playing this roll which aren't seen very much anymore in master play. Let's take a look at them.

He could have tried running all the way with a back man: 24/16. This leaves fewer hitting rolls for White, so on the surface it's a safer play. The problem with the play is that it's unconstructive. If Black is hit, he's accomplished nothing, while even if he's missed, he'll still have the problem of safetying that blot next turn.

Opening Strategy

In *Backgammon for Winners*, I discussed the key goals of the first few moves of the game. The top priority is to make the strong blocking points on your side of the board. For Black, these key points are the 5-point, the 4-point, and the 7-point, in that order. A second key goal (actually just as important as the first) is to make an advanced anchor on the opponent's side of the board; in Black's case, on the 20-point, 21-point, or 18-point. Achieving both of the goals early in the game – an advanced anchor plus one or two key blocking points – virtually guarantees a big early edge.

The strength of 24/18 and 13/11 compared with the running play of 24/16 should now be pretty clear. Playing 24/18 starts a key anchor; playing 13/11 brings a new builder into play for the 5-point and the 7-point. Running with 24/16 doesn't start fighting for **any** key point. That's enough to make it a loser.

Another reasonable play which used to be popular some years ago is simply 13/5, using the whole roll to start the 5-point. While not a bad play, it really requires Black to throw a one next turn to create a good structure. (Assuming he doesn't get hit with a four, of course.) The feeling among today's top players is that playing 24/18 and 13/11 creates a better balanced position, with chances for development on both sides of the board.

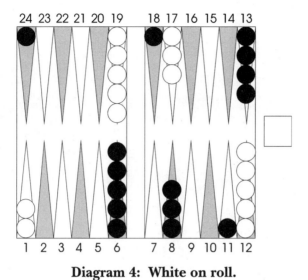

Diagram 4: White on roll.

2. White 55: 17/22(2) 19/24*(2).
A powerful response by White, making two inner-board points while putting Black on the bar.

This is usually the right way to play an early 5-5 if your opponent has split his back men. (If he still has both men on the ace-point, the correct way to play a 5-5 is to move two men from the 13-point to the 3-point.) It puts immediate pressure on Black, who will be doubled if he can't enter his checker from the bar.

3. Black 52: Bar/18.
A good roll by Horan secures the vital defensive anchor, effectively equalizing the position. Now Black can turn his attention to building forward blocking points.

4. White 53: 1/4 12/17.
Not an especially good roll, but White's play is clearly the best available. With the 5, White remakes the 17-point, cleaning up a blot in the process. With the 3, White splits his back men,

trying to make an advanced anchor of his own on the 4-point.

> Here's a good tip to remember: Once your opponent makes an advanced anchor, it becomes even more vital for you to make an anchor of your own.

The reason is simple. Once one side (Black in this game) makes an anchor, White's chances of winning the game by priming Black's back checkers has vanished. However, Black could still win the game by building a prime of his own. To prevent being primed, White must create an anchor of his own, and quickly.

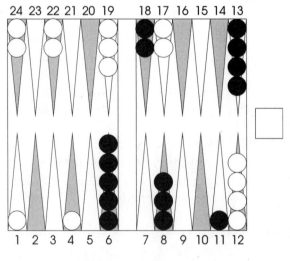

Diagram 5: Black on roll.

5. Black 32: 13/10 6/4*.
A difficult roll with many possible plays. Let's look at some of
the possible alternatives, then see why Horan decided on the
move he actually made.

First Black must decide whether or not to hit on the 4-point with
his deuce. If he doesn't want to hit, he has two plays: the super-
safe 11/6, leaving White no shots, and the reasonably safe 13/
8, leaving White only eight shots (61, 16, 52, 25, 43, 34, 64, and
46). A conservative player might elect to make either of these
plays, but a top player would reject them quickly. Why? Let's
see.

Playing For Flexibility
Top players understand that to build powerful positions, you
must be willing to take reasonable risks. Once in a while, you can
build a strong prime by throwing a series of perfect numbers, but
mostly that won't happen. The dice won't always let you start
games with rolls like 3-1, 4-2, and 5-3, filling in your board. To
create good positions, you've got to be willing to **slot** key points
(place a checker there which you hope to cover the following
turn), and attack your opponent when he moves to the points
you want to build. That's winning backgammon.

Suppose, for instance, that Black plays the super-safe 11/6.
What does White have to be concerned about? He'll be able to
make an advanced anchor with any 3, or to run one of his back
checkers to safety with an 8 or an 11. However, he doesn't have
to do either, since he's under no pressure. As long as Black's
game is completely undeveloped, White can proceed as he
chooses.

Top players understand that the super-safe style leads nowhere.
Instead, they try to put their opponent under pressure to
perform with every single roll.

Now let's look at the merits of Horan's actual play, 6/4* and 13/
10.

Since White is on the bar, he first has to enter. Since he must use half his roll to enter, he won't be able to play his rolls to their full effect. If he enters without hitting, his position becomes very poor very quickly. Black will be able to cover the blot on the 4-point, and he'll be in great position to make the 5-point quickly. White could find himself facing a powerful cube in a turn or two.

In addition, Horan has diversified all his checkers. Instead of big stacks of checkers piled on the 6-point and 13-point, he now has all his checkers in play, preparing to cover or make strong points in the future.

Now suppose White does enter and hit. Black falls further behind in the race, but that's not necessarily so bad. He's quite a bit behind already as a result of White's 5-5 throw, and being a little more behind won't necessarily affect his chances all that much.

> Here's a key secret that top players understand: If you're already substantially behind in the race, it may actually help your chances to fall further behind.

The logic behind this paradoxical insight is that you're likely to lose a straight race in any case, but being further behind may allow you to hold your back points long enough to get a shot or two.

Viewed in this light, Horan's play looks much better than the feeble safe plays. He's taken control of the board and he's dictating the tempo. With a poor roll on White's part, he might win the game in a turn or two.

Before we leave this position, we need to look at one other candidate play: the double-hit, 6/4*/1*. It might seem that if hitting one checker is good, hitting two checkers is even better. Indeed, that's often the case. Here, however, it's not such a strong play. Even if White fails to hit the blot on the 1-point, he still wants to enter both his checkers in Black's home board. The checker on the 1-point will remain a liability in any future exchange of hits, while if Black covers it, he'll have made a point deep in his board and out of play. Top players aren't eager to make the 1-point early in the game. You shouldn't be, either.

6. White 53: Bar/5 1/4*.
Entering with the 5 allows White to hit with the 3, gaining some ground in the race. A good throw for White.

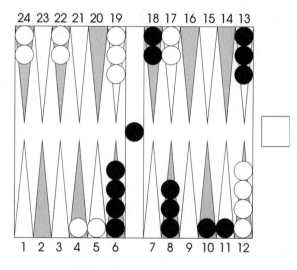

Diagram 6: Black on roll.

7. Black 64: Bar/21 11/5*.
Entering on the 21-point is forced, after which Horan has a choice between hitting on the 5-point or hitting on the 4-point. Since the 5-point is more valuable than the 4-point, Horan hits on the 5.

Why is the 5-point more valuable? Look at it this way. If Black makes the 5-point, and White anchors on the 4-point, White's checkers are obstructed behind three blocking points (the 5-point, 6-point, and 8-points). On the other hand, if Black makes the 4-point and White anchors on the 5-point, White's checkers are not nearly so blocked. In general, you should try to make your points in order: first the 5-point, then the 4-point, then the 3-point, and so on.

8. White 61: Bar/1 4/10*.
White can't hit the blot on the 5-point, but he picks off the blot on the 10-point instead.

9. Black 64: Bar/21 13/7.
Making the 21-point gives Black two strong defensive anchors as a fallback position. It will be very difficult for White to move his checkers past those two points without leaving some shots later on. With the 6, Black simply slots the next good point, in this case the 7-point.

10. White 43: 1/5* 12/15.
Hitting with the 4 is certainly clear, but the three is awkward. White could make a safe play by moving 19/22, but that puts a valuable builder out of play. On the 19-point, the checker is a builder for both the valuable 20-point and the less valuable 23-point. On the 22-point, the checker is a builder only for the 23-point.

Instead, White starts the 15-point with one of the spares on the midpoint. Risky? Not really. Since Black is on the bar, he doesn't have many numbers that both enter and hit. In addition, White would have no difficulty reentering a checker since Black hasn't yet begun to build his home board.

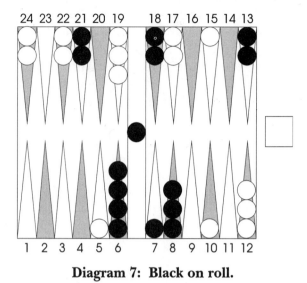

24 23 22 21 20 19   18 17 16 15 14 13

1 2 3 4 5 6   7 8 9 10 11 12

Diagram 7: Black on roll.

11. Black 63: Stays out.

Black would have liked to enter, but staying out isn't too serious. He should be able to reenter next turn.

Should White double? No. In order to double, you need to have both a very solid advantage and some threats which, if executed, will force your opponent to drop a later double. This is known as **losing your market**. If you can't lose your market, that is, if your best won't be enough to make your opponent give up later, then you shouldn't double yet.

In this position, White has an advantage, but it's not going to change very much from turn to turn. A good result for White would be to safety a couple of his blots. Black will then most likely enter his checker from the bar. At that point, if White doubled, Black would have a very clear take. So there's no reason for White to double now.

12. White 41: 12/16 15/16.

The 16-point should be a useful landing spot as White tries to maneuver his checkers toward the home board. He could have made the 15-point instead (10/15), but the 16-point is better. Sometime in the near future, White will have to clear his outside blocking points and bring the checkers into the inner board. Points closer to the home board are easier to clear than points farther away. Hence the 16-point is preferred to the 15-point.

Excellent play by Pauen.

13. Black 21: Bar/23 8/7.

Black enters with the 2 and finally makes a new offensive point with his ace.

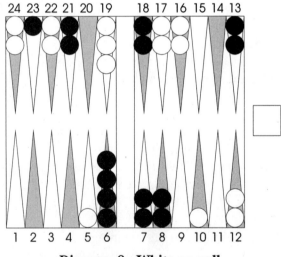

Diagram 8: White on roll.

14. White 52: 5/12.

Pauen runs a checker to safety. He could also have safetied a checker with 15/8, but his actual play was better.

> The player who is ahead in the race should try to disengage from the back.

By moving the rearmost checker first, Pauen keeps his formation compact and better coordinated.

If White had tried 15/8 instead, his rear checker would be subject to attack, and even if it survived the attack, White would be a big underdog to get the checker to safety. Notice that if Black misses this three-shot, White should be able to pick up the blot on the 10-point without much difficulty.

15. Black 21: 13/10*.
Horan has a choice here. He could build the most valuable point in his home board by moving 7/5 6/5. There's not much point to a strong blocking position, however, if there aren't any enemy checkers to block. Horan correctly sends a White checker back home.

> Given a choice between hitting and building, hitting will take precedence in most (but not all) situations.

16. White 63: Bar/9.
White enters and hops Black's small blockade.

Some might ask, "Why not the attacking play, Bar/3 and 17/23*?" The answer is that White doesn't need to attack here. He's already got a good position with a big lead in the race. What he needs to do is get his back checker to safety, so that he doesn't have to worry about Black building a prime in front of him. Once that problem is taken care of, White can concentrate on filling in his 23-point and 20-point. Note that when the attacking play fails, White's advantage evaporates immediately.

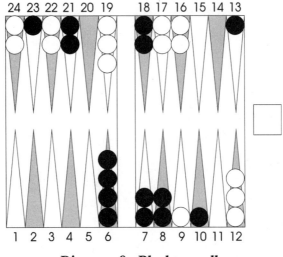

Diagram 9: Black on roll.

17. Black 64: 13/9* 10/4.

Hitting with the 4 is clear-cut. The play of the 6, however, presents a difficult choice. Horan could try 21/15, aiming to control the outfield. If his blots survived, he could follow up by making the 9-point or the 10-point, extending his growing prime.

The problem with that play, however, is that Black would have left himself very exposed. With five blots strewn around and no anchor in White's home board, a lucky hit by White could knock Black out of the game on the very next roll. That's too big a risk to take, especially since Black's two defensive anchors give him excellent long-term chances.

Instead, Horan makes the veteran's choice: he calmly slots his 4-point, aiming for a small gain if White misses this shot, while risking very little if White hits.

18. White 51: Bar/1 12/17.
White misses and can't escape, so he is content to bring a builder to bear on the key 20-point. White's game will improve greatly if he can fill in that vital landing spot.

19. Black 52: 23/18 6/4.
An excellent roll. Black covers the blot in the most efficient way, with a deuce, while with the 5 he moves his rear blot to a position where he can bring it around to the 9, 10, or 11-point next turn. Black has four checkers committed to holding the two anchors for several more turns, and he needs all the rest of his checkers working to strengthen his growing prime.

20. White 55: 12/22(2).
Essentially a forced play. With the loss of the midpoint, White's rear checker is getting stranded. White will need to extricate it very quickly.

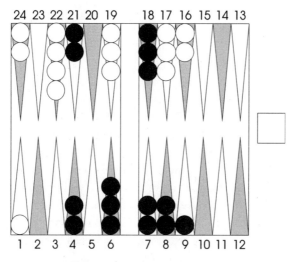

Diagram 10: Black on roll.

21. Black 21: 7/5 6/5.

An imaginative play by Horan. He'd like to move his spare checker on the 18-point around to join in the battle for the 5-point, but unfortunately, it's blocked. He could play safe with a move like 9/6 or 9/7 8/7. Instead, however, he deliberately opens up the 7-point to make the 5-point! What's his idea?

Horan recognizes that he has too few checkers on the scene to neatly make a **5-point prime** (five points in a row) by waiting to throw just the right numbers. By filling in the 5-point, he uses the few checkers he has to maximum advantage. If White doesn't immediately throw a 6, Horan can cover the 7-point next turn with any 2, creating a very strong position.

And what if White does roll a 6? That's a calculated risk, of course, but in that case Horan will fall back on his primary game plan – using the anchors on the 21 and 18-points to generate a winning shot late in the game.

22. White 65: 1/7*/12.

White throws the 6 and pops into the outfield. Black will have to win from his holding position after all.

23. Black 44: Bar/21 18/6.

Horan enters and brings another spare to bear on the 3-point, the next point he wants to make.

Should White double now? Not quite. If White is able to move his checker on the 12-point to safety this turn, say with a roll of 6-1 (12/19) he'll be in an ideal position to double. Black would still have a take based on his chances of hitting a game-winning shot later in the game. However, there's a considerable chance that White will not be able to safety that checker. In particular, all of the following throws would leave that checker in jeopardy: 66, 33, 62, 63, and 21. That's a total of 9 out of a possible 36 dice throws, or 25%! White's proper strategy is to move the checker to safety, then offer a perfectly-timed double. Pauen correctly leaves the cube in the middle.

24. White 52: 12/19.
A good throw. The checker moves to safety, and is usefully placed to make the 5-point.

25. Black 21: 9/7 8/7.
Horan makes four points in a row. Equally good was 6/3, starting the 3-point.

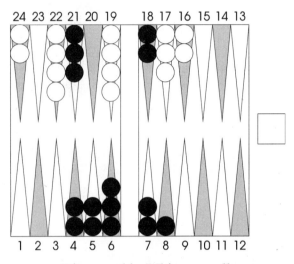

Diagram 11: White on roll.

White could reasonably double now, but he chooses to wait one more turn.

26. White 51: 17/23.
White can't clear either outside point, so he moves the odd checker to the 2-point.

27. Black 42: 8/2.
Black really wants to make the 3-point next, but this roll is particularly awkward.

> In general, when you're building your board and waiting for a shot, you want to slot and cover your points in order, from the highest to the lowest.

That's an excellent rule, but here slotting the 3-point involves breaking the 7-point. Horan decides that's too high a price to pay, so he keeps the 7-point and slots the 2-point instead.

My preference would be to play 7/3 and 6/4. I'd be willing to loosen my position for one turn since it's unlikely that I will get a shot immediately. (On White's next roll, only 64 forces him to leave a blot.) Since I probably won't get a winning shot for two turns, I should have time to cover the 3-point.

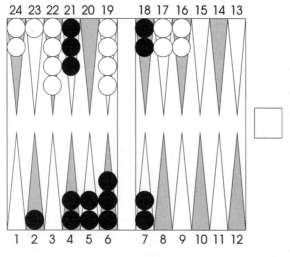

Diagram 12: White on roll.

28. White doubles to 2.
A perfectly-timed double by White. If he waits until he clears the 17-point or the 16-point, Black would definitely have a pass. As it stands, Black is faced with a very difficult decision.

29. Black takes.
A difficult choice for Horan. Let's take a look at the considerations that govern the decision to take or drop.

When To Take A Double

The race is a factor in most cube decisions, but here the race is a foregone conclusion. The **pip count** (the number of pips that each side must throw to bear off all checkers) is 74 for White and 151 for Black. Black is not going to win any races.

If Black can't win the race, then he's going to have to win by first hitting a shot, then containing the checker. His chances of getting a shot are actually quite good. Barring doubles, White has only six numbers to clear the 16-point (31, 13, 61, 16, 63 and 36) and six other numbers to clear the 17-point (65, 56, 62, 26, 52, and 25). If White clears the 17-point before clearing the 16-point, then his chances of clearing the 16-point without leaving a shot are very small.

If White leaves a shot on the 16-point, Black will actually be a favorite to hit it! He'd be able to hit with any 5 or any 2, plus a combination shot like 41. Overall, Black would have about a 60% chance to hit a blot on the 16-point or the 17-point. (That's the great advantage of holding two anchors). And of course, even if White clears the 16 and 17-points, he might still lose by leaving a blot on the 19-point.

How often does Black need to win this position in order to take a double? In my first book, *Backgammon for Winners*, I explained that if Black can't lose a gammon, he would need to win at least one game in four to take a double. Why only one in four? Let's quickly review why that's the case.

Suppose this position came up four consecutive times, and Black dropped all four games. In that case he would lose four points. If he took all four games, however, and managed to win only one while losing three, he would lose six points in the three games he lost while winning back two points in the game he won. The result? A net loss of four points, just as before. So one win in four games is the break-even point for taking a double if you can't get gammoned. If you can win more than one game in four, you can certainly take, while if your chances are less than that, you should pass.

In the position we're looking at, Black can certainly win more than one game in four. He's a favorite to get at least one shot, while he might get as many as two or three shots. Hitting a shot, however, doesn't guarantee victory. Black would still have to contain the checker he hits, and while he's likely to do that, White will have some chances to escape. My guess is that Black can win this position about 35% of the time.

So Black has a clear take, right? Not so fast! There's one other factor to consider – the gammon factor.

The Gammon Factor

If Black can lose a gammon, he will need to win more than his usual 25% of the time to justify a take. How much more? That depends on his estimate of how likely he is to be gammoned. Here's a rule that covers this situation:

> For every two gammons that you are in danger of losing, you need to win one additional game to break even.

To see why this rule makes sense, look at what happens when you exchange a single loss for either a gammon loss or a turnaround win. If the cube is on two, losing a single game costs you two points, while losing a gammon costs you four points. Losing a gammon costs you two additional points compared to a single game loss. If the cube is on two and you win a single game, instead of losing, you have a two point gain instead of a two point loss. Your net gain is actually four points. To summarize: turning a loss into a win gains you four points; turning a loss into a gammon costs you two points. So two gammon losses balance out one extra win.

This insight gives us a tool for taking the cube in positions where we might get gammoned. Suppose we were thinking about taking a double and we estimated that we might get gammoned 20% of the time. In that case, we'd need 10% extra wins to balance the 20% gammons. So instead of needing to win the position 25% of the time, we'd actually need to have 25% plus 10%, or 35% wins, to take.

Now let's get back to Horan's actual position. Certainly it's possible for Horan to lose a gammon in this position. He's got a good chance of getting a shot, but he might never get a shot, or he might miss the shots he gets. If he hits a shot he'll almost certainly save the gammon if he doesn't win the game, but if he misses his shots, he's got a reasonable chance of being gammoned. One way to estimate his chances of losing a gammon is to compare the number of pips that White has to roll to bear off with the number of pips that Black has to roll to get all his checkers into his home board. We figured out White's total already when we did our pip count; it's 74 pips to bear off.

To figure out Black's total, compute the number of pips that each of Black's outer-board checkers must move to reach Black's 6-point. This gives us a measure of the minimum amount of pippage Black must throw to get all checkers into his inner board, ready to bear off. In this position, the three checkers on the 21-point must move 15 pips each, the two checkers on the 18-point must move 12 pips each, and the two checkers on the 7-point require one pip each. That's a grand total of 45 plus 24 plus 2, or 71 pips, just short of White's bear-off total.

What this calculation tells us is that if Black does not hit a shot as White is bearing in, he is about even money to save the gammon.

Putting all this information together, we can make an educated guess about the likely outcomes of the game.

- Black has excellent chances to get at least one shot and might get as many as two. His winning chances are better than 30%, perhaps as high as 40%.

- If Black can win 40% of the time, White will win at least 60%. If White wins 60%, about half his wins will be gammons, or about 30% gammons and 30% single wins.

- If White can win a gammon 30% of the time, Black needs 15% extra wins, about his basic 25%, to take. That means he needs 40% wins, total.

What all this means is that an optimistic estimate of Black's possibilities yields 40% wins for Black, 30% gammon losses, and 30% single losses, which in turn is just a bare take. That's cutting it a little close for my taste, and Black quite possibly might not do as well as 40% wins. I would opt to pass. Horan elects to take, a not uncharacteristic decision for him. He's a courageous and tenacious player who likes to force his opponent to earn his points. Correct or not, Horan's decision means the game will end with an interesting and possibly dramatic fight.

30. White 31: 16/17 16/19.
An excellent shot, clearing the difficult 9-point. If White doubled now, Black would surely pass.

31. Black 63: 21/15 6/3.
Hopping out with the 6 is clear, since Black needs that checker to build his blockade. Since Black wants as powerful a board as possible if and when White leaves a shot, he starts to build the

3-point with his 3.

32. White 11: 19/20(2) 22/23(2).
Another great shot for White, filling in the gap on the 20-point. This greatly increases the number of rolls that will eventually clear the 17-point successfully. Black is in serious trouble after White's last two rolls, and he has to start moving quickly to save the gammon.

33. Black 22: 15/11 7/3.
Not a bad roll, making the 3-point.

34. White 66: 17/23(3) 19/off.
White's third great roll in a row. Now Black's chances of hitting a shot are very small, while his chances of being gammoned are very real.

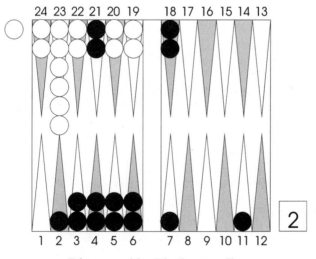

Diagram 13: Black on roll.

35. Black 61: 18/12 7/6.
Much better than making Black's 1-point. Saving the gammon is the overwhelming priority.

How To Save A Gammon

> Remember this rule: When racing to save the gammon, try to bring all your outfield checkers to the 6-point. This will ensure that you waste the minimum number of pips. Also, try to cross over from quadrant to quadrant if possible.

Black's last play achieved two crossovers, and also moved a checker to the 6-point.

36. White 62: 19/off 23/off.
Disaster strikes! After three great rolls, White throws the only number that would force him to leave a shot. To play backgammon successfully, you have to have the mental toughness to adjust to these sudden swings of fortune. Of course, Horan only has a 30% chance to hit this shot (Black hits with any deuce, which is a total of 11 rolls out of 36), but ...

37. Black 52: 21/19* 18/13.
Black hits! Now it's a whole new game. Black's job now will be to cover the 2-point very soon, followed by making the 7-point. If he can make a full 6-point prime, or get very close to that, he'll be able to turn the cube to 4 and double White out.

White's job is simple: enter and escape before Black can build his prime.

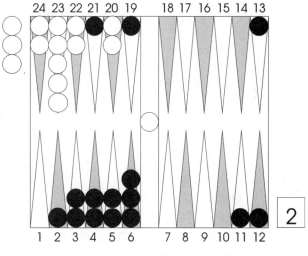

Diagram 14: White on roll.

38. White 11: Bar/2* 20/21*(2).
White follows up his awful roll last turn with a great shot this turn! Note that White had some really bad numbers. Throwing 13 or 14, for instance, resulted in White's entering on the 1-point and breaking the 20-point, exposing another blot.

Now Black is again in danger of being gammoned.

39. Black 62: Bar/19.
Entering one man is a reasonably good throw for Black.

40. White 62: 2/10.
White hops into the outfield, taking aim at all Black's juicy blots. Black now has 13 chances (out of 36) to hit: 61, 62, 63, 51, 52, 53, and 55.

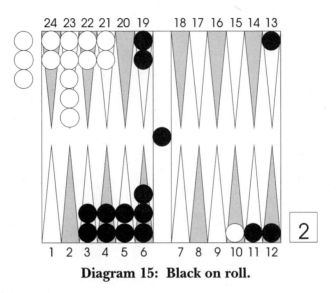

Diagram 15: Black on roll.

41. Black 63: Bar/19 13/10*.
Black hits and is back in control. Another huge swing!

42. White 32: Bar/2 21/24.
White enters but breaks his board, which weakens his chances. Black can now hit with less chance that he may end up trapped on the bar.

Should Black be thinking about doubling? Not yet. White still has good chances of escaping Black's blockade and running home, and he might even be able to still win a gammon with a lucky throw. The time to double will come later.

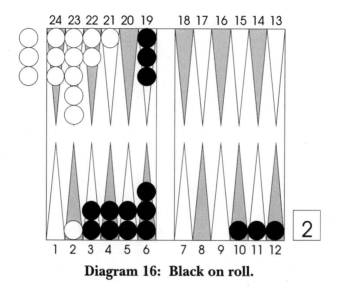

Diagram 16: Black on roll.

43. Black 11: 19/18 10/9 3/2*(2).
Black could have used this whole roll to hit loose on the 2-point (6/2*) but his actual play is better. He has good control of the outfield and no immediate targets for White to shoot at. Note too that not hitting White at all is not an option. Black must prevent White from getting into the outfield, if he can.

44. White stays out.
Black's making progress, but he still needs to close the 3-point before he can double.

45. Black 53: 18/13 12/9.
Nice play by Horan. His outfield coverage is now excellent while he's blocked White's potential winning number of 36.

46. White stays out.

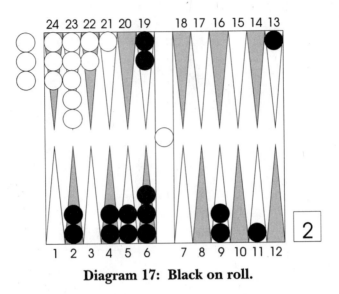

Diagram 17: Black on roll.

47. Black 63: 9/3 6/3.
A great shot. Now Black is on the verge of doubling.

48. White stays out.

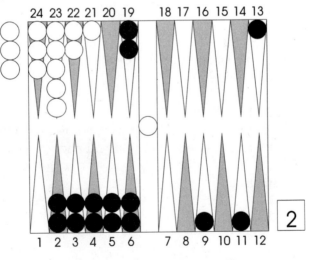

Diagram 18: Black on roll.

49. Black redoubles to 4.
A very clear double now.

50. White passes.
Can White possibly take this double? Let's see.

Next turn Black will either make his 7-point (if he rolls some combination of 2s, 4s, and 6s) or slot his 7-point by sticking a blot there, hoping to cover next turn. White will have one chance to escape by rolling a 1-6, after which Black will make the 7-point. Once he has six points in a row, it's an easy matter for Black to close his board: He just has to move his spares into his home board, slot his 1-point, and cover it. If Black gets hit in this process, it's no problem: He just reenters his spare, brings it around, and tries again.

Since it's extremely likely that Black will close out the single White checker in this position, what we really need to know is this: What is the chance that White can win the game if he is closed out, given that he already has three men off?

That's a question which backgammon theoreticians have already figured out. The answer is 11%. That's not close to the 25% that White needs to take a double, so he correctly passes.

Incidentally, you may want to memorize the following little table. It shows White's winning chances in positions similar to this one when he has a checker closed out but some number of men off.

Number of men White has borne off	White's Winning chances
No men off	2%
One man off	5%
Two men off	8%
Three men off	11%
Four men off	16%
Five men off	25%

These situations come up fairly frequently, and the knowledge contained in this table may make (or save) you a lot of money. Learn it!

Summary

An early set of double-fives by Pauen pins Horan in a defensive position. Horan takes some reasonable chances to improve his front game, but when these fail, he reaches a holding position with his opponent's 21-point and 18-point.

After hitting a checker later, Horan takes extraordinary chances to try to build a prime quickly, knowing that he can always fall back on his holding position later. Pauen finally escapes, and offers a powerful double a couple of turns later.

Horan makes a daring but questionable take, and Pauen rolls very well to eliminate most, but not all, of Horan's chances. Horan finally hits a desperation shot on the 19-point, and eventually fills in the last key point in his board. With only three checkers off, Pauen has to pass Horan's eventual recube to 4.

Two aspects of this game repay close study. The first is Horan's aggressiveness in trying to build his board when he has the security of two defensive anchors. The second is Horan's placement of his pieces to control the outfield after hitting his last shot. His control pays off as he is able to catch Pauen's last checker coming around.

6

Wilcox Snellings emerged on the backgammon scene in 1988 and was immediately recognized as one of the world's top players. In the balloting to determine the rankings of the world's best, he was voted #1 in 1993 and #2 in 1995. His most recent major win was the Las Vegas tournament of 1995.

Paul Magriel is one of the all-time legends of backgammon. He won the second tournament he ever entered – the Aruba tourney of 1971 - and he's been winning major tournaments ever since. His major victories include back-to-back Children's Hospital tourneys in 1974-75, the World Championship in 1978, back-to-back Bahamas Pro-Ams in 1994-95, and the World Cup Consolation in 1996. He's also the author of the classic book *Backgammon*, which taught a generation of players about the elements of backgammon strategy.

This game was played in an early round of the Las Vegas Open in 1991. It's a match to 11 points, and right now the score is Snellings 9, Magriel 8.

In this game we'll see several examples of strategic ideas that we haven't seen before – checker and cube decisions that are heavily influenced by the match score.

In the early stages of a match, with many points to go for each side, cube and checker play tends to look just like money play. At the later stages of a match, with just a few points left for one side or the other, players have to take the score into consideration. Let's see just how this works for our two combatants.

Playing To The Score

At this score, Magriel needs 3 points to win the match, while Snellings needs only 2. Magriel's doubling strategy is not very different from a normal money game, or from a situation early in a match. His doubles get a bonus in this situation, since if he gives a cube and Snellings accepts, Snellings will never redouble. (Winning two points is sufficient to win the match for him). The terminology for this is that Snellings will own a **dead cube.**

To see why this is advantageous for Magriel, imagine that Magriel doubles and Snellings accepts. Now imagine that Snellings turns the game around and becomes, say, an 80% favorite. In a money game, Snellings would always win in this situation, since he would double and Magriel would pass. But at this score, Snellings must play these games out to the finish. Since Snellings is "only" 80% to win, Magriel will pull a few of these games out in a last-minute turnaround.

There's a compensating slight downside for Magriel, however, in that his gammons don't work for him as well as in a money game. If he wins a gammon, he can win only three points instead of the usual four. The net result is that Magriel can double slightly sooner than in a money game, but not by very much.

If Snellings gets the early advantage, his strategy is quite a bit different from normal. First of all, if Snellings doubles and Magriel takes, Magriel will redouble to four automatically. (Since Snellings needs only two points to win the match, Magriel would lose the match if he lost the game with the cube on two, so he might as well put it on four.) But notice that if Snellings wins a gammon with the cube centered on one, he wins the match outright. This implies that if Snellings gets an early advantage with some gammon chances, he's usually right to go for an undoubled gammon rather than double at all. In fact, that's exactly the scenario we'll see in this game.

1. White 21: 12/14 19/20
White starts his all-important 5-point (the 20-point in the diagram) while unstacking the midpoint. This is the preferred method of starting the game with a 21 for almost all the world's top players. If Black doesn't roll a 4, White will make the 5-point and be off to an early edge. If Black does hit, White is at least guaranteed a complex game.

A play which has become popular in recent years, especially among weaker players on the tournament circuit, is 12/14 1/2. White declines to slot the 20-point and, by splitting, makes slotting difficult for the opponent. Although this might be objectively as strong as Magriel's play, it has a great drawback – it creates much simpler positions, where it's hard to outplay your opponent.

> If you want to make a mark in the backgammon world, learn how to create and master complicated positions. It's the road to success.

2. Black 65: 24/13
Correct. There's nothing better to do with this roll than simply run to the midpoint. I've seen some players try 24/18 13/8, but that's overplaying the position.

> Take what the dice give you. Don't try for too much.

Escaping a checker in the opening is a simple but useful objective.

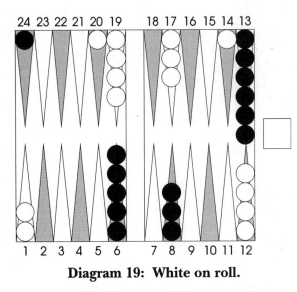

Diagram 19: White on roll.

3. White 41: 19/20 1/5

Covering the 20-point with the ace is of course completely clear. The play of the four offers a couple of options. Magriel's play. 1/5, spreads out the rear checkers to cover the whole board, making it difficult for Snellings to play safely next turn.

My own preference is for 12/16. This play maximizes White's building chances in the area of the board where White already has an advantage. I think this is the play most likely to lead to a quick knockout. Both plays have their merits, however, and this is really a stylistic question.

4. Black 64: 24/14*

An excellent shot, escaping the last checker while hitting at the same time. Early edge to Snellings.

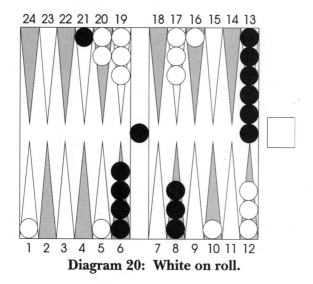

Diagram 20: White on roll.

5. White 22: Bar/4 12/14*/16
A great comeback, entering, hitting, and building.

The first two deuces, Bar/2 and 12/14*, are clearly forced. With the last two, I prefer 1/5, building a solid anchor, to Magriel's play 2/4 and 14/16. Magriel's play offers more flexibility and more future good rolls; the other play offers a solid asset for the rest of the game.

6. Black 42: Bar/21 6/4*
The only safe play here, Bar/21 and 8/6, is hopeless, leaving Black with no position and White with a fully developed game and plenty of attacking chances.

> In the opening, you must actively fight for equality, rather than play passively, hoping to survive.

If White throws poorly, Black will be poised to make a second point and get right back into the game.

7. White 64: Bar/4*/10
A good shot, hitting and leaping into the outfield.

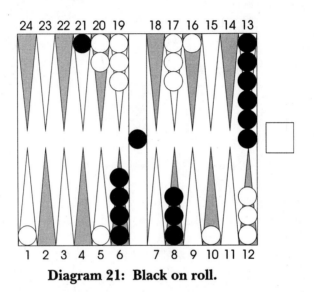

Diagram 21: Black on roll.

Importance of Connectivity

Although Magriel has several blots spread around the board, notice how his checkers support each other. The checker on the 16-point is guarded by the checkers on the 12-point and the 10-point. The checker on the 10 is guarded by the checker on the 5, which in turn is guarded by the checker on the 1-point. No matter which blot Black is able to hit, White will have at least a single return shot. This connectivity is the mark of well thought-out development.

8. Black 33: Bar/22 8/5*(2) 13/10*
Unless this happens! Doubles from the bar in the early game will usually turn the game around, and that's the case here. With two enemy checkers on the bar and another blot to shoot at, Black is firmly in control.

Should White have tried to guard against this possibility? Absolutely not. In the opening you're trying to build solid yet flexible positions, taking into account your opponent's most likely rolls.

> Trying to guard against the 35-1 long shots will only drive you into a cramped and ultimately losing style of play. Don't fall into that trap.

9. White 43: Bar/4 Bar/3
Forced.

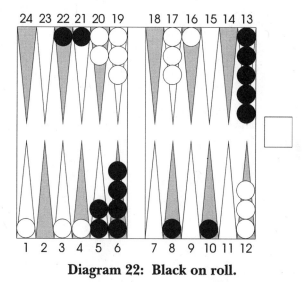

Diagram 22: Black on roll.

Is this a double for Black? No. Both sides have a two-point board and four blots. Black has a nice edge since he's on roll, but it's still too soon to double.

10. Black 64: 10/4* 8/4

A first-rate play by Snellings. There was a tempting alternative of 8/4* 22/16* hitting two men, but Snelling's play is better. After the double hit, Snellings would lose all of his advantage if Magriel then reentered with a four. Snellings play illustrates a key principle:

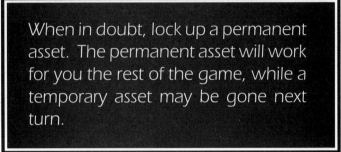

> When in doubt, lock up a permanent asset. The permanent asset will work for you the rest of the game, while a temporary asset may be gone next turn.

11. White 62: Bar/2 16/22*

White must hit to keep Black off balance.

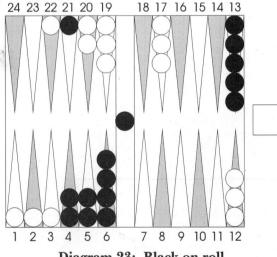

Diagram 23: Black on roll.

12. Black 42: Bar/21 13/11
With the four, Black locks up a permanent asset. With the two,
he begins to develop the checkers on the midpoint. Good play.

13. White 63: 2/11*
A strong hit, and of course White had no other constructive play.

14. Black 32: Bar/22* 13/11*
A fine shot. Black is firmly in control of the game again.

15. White stays out.
A dreadful number for White. Should Black double?

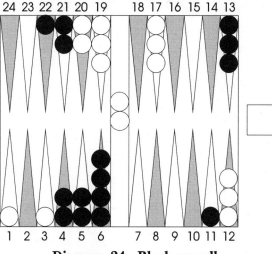

Diagram 24: Black on roll.

The answer is no. This might surprise many players who are used
to money play but not tournament play. Let's see why Black does
better to leave the cube in the middle.

Playing For An Undoubled Gammon

What makes this position so strong for Black is not that he will
win almost all the games, but that many, if not most, of his wins
will be gammons. By leaving the cube in the middle, he will win
the game and the match when he scores a gammon win.

(Remember, Black needs only two points to win the match, while White needs three.) On the other hand, when White enters quickly from the bar and turns the game around, he'll only win one point, just equalizing the score.

> If you have good chances to win a gammon, and you're just two points away from the match, it's almost always right to leave the cube alone and try to win an undoubled gammon.

So Black's correct strategy is to leave the cube alone, attack White's blots, and try to achieve a blitz closeout or at least pin White in an ace-point game or a deuce-point game, which will still offer good gammon chances.

Suppose Black goes ahead and doubles anyway. Should White give up the game in that case?

Interestingly, White should take quickly! This might seem counterintuitive at first. If Black's game is so strong that he should play for a gammon, how could White be thinking about taking? To see why, we have to consider the match score again.

Suppose Black doubles and White drops. Black will then lead in the 11-point match by a score of 10 points to 8, and the next game will be the Crawford game, when White will not be able to double. In order to win the match, White will have to win the Crawford game, making the score Black 10 - White 9, and then double and win the next game. In other words, White will have to win two straight games to win the match. If the players are evenly matched, White's chances of winning one game are just 50%, so his chances of winning two straight are 25%.

On the other hand, suppose Black doubles this game and White takes and immediately redoubles to four. Then the match will be decided by whoever wins or loses this game, with gammons being irrelevant. Are White's chances better than 25% in that case. Yes indeed! In fact, I would estimate White's raw winning chances in this position to be in the 30-35% range. White will often make an ace-point, deuce-point, or 3-point game, and sometimes he will develop a full backgame. There will also be games where Black's attack simply fails outright and White is able to win by building a prime of his own. Overall, playing for the match right here would be by far White's best choice.

16. Black 53: 13/8 6/3*
Playing for a gammon, Black naturally attacks on the 3-point and brings up the reserves.

17. White 43: Bar/3*
A good shot, slowing down Black's momentum.

18. Black 52: Bar/23 8/3*
The attack continues.

19. White stays out.

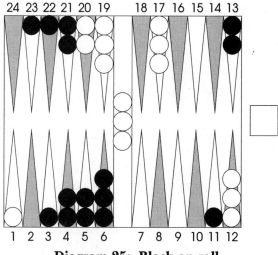

Diagram 25: Black on roll.

20. Black 51: 13/7
White gets a lucky break as Black fails to cover the 3-point.
Black's play not only brings a new cover number for the 3-point,
but prepares to make the bar if the attack slows down.

21. White stays out.

22. Black 42: 7/3 11/9
With the 3-point made, Black next takes aim at the 2-point or the
7-point. The 2-point is more important right now, but, being
farther away from Black's spare checkers, it will be more difficult
to make.

23. White 21: Bar/1 Bar/2
A great shot! If Magriel can enter his last checker quickly, the
game may start to turn around.

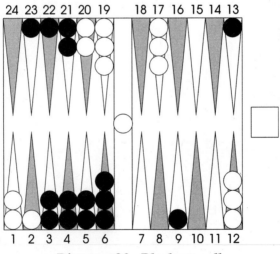

Diagram 26: Black on roll.

24. Black 65: 13/2*
Black continues the assault on the 2-point.

25. White 32: Bar/2*
Another good roll for White. Black's attack is rapidly running out of steam.

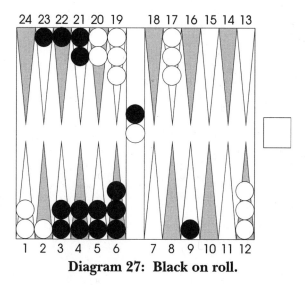

Diagram 27: Black on roll.

26. Black 64: Bar/15
A strong and subtle play by Snellings. If the battle is now for the 2-point, one might reasonably expect Black to play 9/3 with his 6, bringing another attacker within direct range of the 2-point. Snellings, however, sees that he is now very unlikely to win the battle for the 2-point, and a checker placed on the 3-point might be in danger of playing little role in the rest of the game. By leaving the checker on the 9-point, it has the potential of later making the now more valuable 7-point. This is the kind of subtle yet deadly accurate play that separates the world-class professional from the merely talented amateur.

27. White 31: Bar/1 12/15*

28. Black stays out.
A very big swing on the last two rolls. The position is now starting to swing in Magriel's favor.

29. White 64: 17/23* 19/23
Very strong roll. White makes another inner point while putting a second Black checker on the bar.

30. Black stays out.

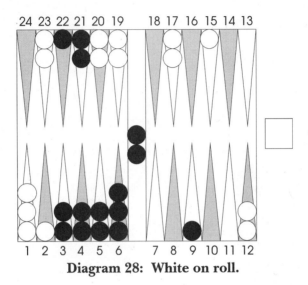

Diagram 28: White on roll.

31. White doubles to 2.
The game has turned completely around in the last three turns. Now it's Black that has two men on the bar with more vulnerable blots in danger. As we say, "That's backgammon!" The nature of the game is such that massive sudden swings of fortune are relatively commonplace.

> The good player must have the fortitude to adjust to these swings without losing composure or control.

Building that mental mindset is as much a part of becoming a top player as mastering when to slot a point or break a prime.

Back to our actual position. As I said in the introduction to this game, White's doubling strategy in this situation is more or less the same according to normal strategy principles. He can profit from a gammon, although not as much as in a money game. (A gammon here only earns him one extra point rather than two.) This is a reasonable money double with two Black checkers on the bar, so White sends the cube over.

32. Black takes.
Also reasonable. Black has an advanced anchor (the 21-point) and a strong home board with some White checkers blocked. If White doesn't throw a 5 or a 6 this turn and Black enters a checker, he should be in good shape.

33. White 55: 17/22*(2) 23/18 12/17
A great shot, in fact White's best number. Three of his fives are clear: making the 22-point on Black's head and hopping out to the 7-point from behind Black's prime. The last five, however, might seem unusual to some players. Why play 12/17, exposing himself to a roll of 44 by Black, instead of safely playing 15/20?

The answer is that White recognizes that he's not going to be able to get all his men home before Black finally reenters from the bar. In that case, he's going to need some steppingstones in the outfield to get home safely, and the 17-point rates to be a very useful steppingstone. So White starts the point now.

34. Black 54: Bar/21
There's nothing Black can do for now but roll and hope for the best. If he enters fairly quickly, he can get back in the game. If he dances for several turns, the game could be all over.

35. White 42: 7/9*/13
White now has triple coverage for the 17-point, which is his next goal.

36. Black 42: Bar/21

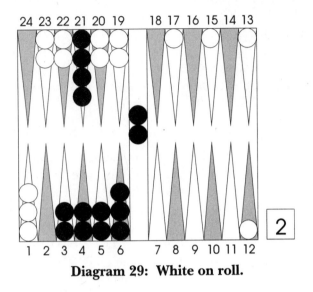

Diagram 29: White on roll.

37. White 66: 1/7(3) 12/18
A tremendous shot, getting all of his men out from behind Black's blockade. White's now in excellent shape. With his last six, he starts the 18-point. If he can make the 17 and 18-point before Black enters, he should be able to get home with ease.

38. Black stays out.

39. White 21: 13/15 17/18

40. Black 41: Bar/24 Bar/21
A great roll! With all checkers in, Black can now threaten to hit any loose blots that White chooses to leave.

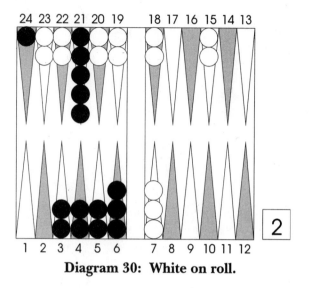

Diagram 30: White on roll.

41. White 21: 7/10

White begins to maneuver his men on the 7-point home. The other play, 7/9 7/8, gives better outfield coverage but leaves too many blots in case something goes wrong.

42. Black 33: 24/21 6/3 5/2(2)

A bad throw. Black gets squeezed and the first crack appears in his home board.

43. White 41: 7/11 10/11

White's checkers piggyback their way toward home.

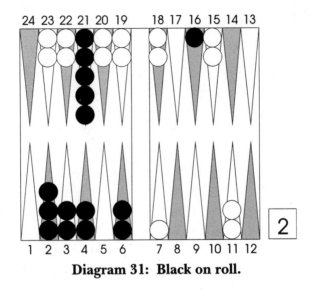

24 23 22 21 20 19   18 17 16 15 14 13

2

1 2 3 4 5 6   7 8 9 10 11 12

Diagram 31: Black on roll.

44. Black 51: 21/16 3/2
Black could play safe with something like 6/1 3/2, but that's an awful play. With his home board shattered, Black would have little or no chance of winning even if he hit a lucky shot later. Snellings correctly contests the outfield while he still has a threatening board.

45. White 65: 11/16*/22
Hits and goes to safety. With the game mostly won, White has no need to leave extra shots in the outfield. From now on, it's correct for him to play as safely as possible.

46. Black stays out.

47. White 51: 7/13
Moves closer to home while keeping double coverage of the vital 16 and 17-points.

48. Black 64: Bar/21 No 6

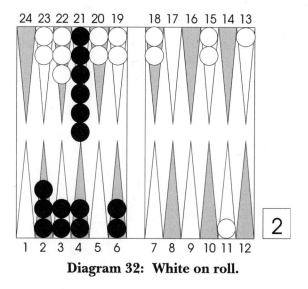

Diagram 32: White on roll.

49. White 51: 13/19

Now that Black is in from the bar, White has to be very careful leaving blots around. Since he can't safety the checker on the 11-point with this roll, he picks up the checker on the 13 instead.

50. Black 44: 21/17(4)

A great shot. White is still a substantial favorite, but clearing the 15-point in a roll or two may prove more difficult than expected. Meanwhile, the checker on the 11-point is now under direct attack. Actually, it's not as easy to safety that checker as you might imagine...

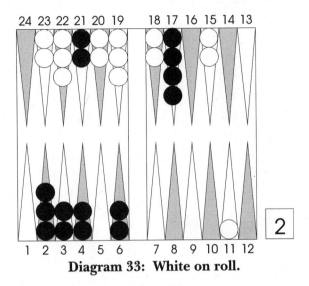

Diagram 33: White on roll.

51. White 21: 11/13 19/20

Oops. White has to leave a direct shot. In fact, 11 of White's 36 numbers failed to get that checker to safety. (21, 12, 51, 15, 32, 23, 64, 46, 66, 33, and 55.)

Although White has to leave a direct shot, he does have a choice of where to leave the shot. Most players would automatically move 11/14, bringing the checker closer to home. Magriel makes the better play, 11/13 19/20. Do you see why leaving the checker on the 13-point is better?

White's first priority is playing the roll as safely as possible. Moving 11/14 allows Black to hit with 15 numbers: all threes (11 numbers) plus 52, 25, 12 and 21. Moving 11/13 19/20 also gives Black 15 hitters: all fours plus 53, 35, 13, and 31. So in terms of immediate safety the two plays are equivalent.

The next consideration is to see if either play gives Black an awkward number to play. Here there is a difference. If White plays 11/14, any Black roll which does not hit can be played safely by moving off the 17-point. But if White plays 11/13,

Black has a problem with the roll of 21. Black won't want to leave a direct shot with 17/14 (he might get gammoned if he got hit), so instead he will weaken his board a little by playing 3/1 2/1. That's not a big concession, but there's no reason that White shouldn't try for that sequence. Accurate play by Magriel.

52. Black 51: 17/11
Black misses, so he starts to move builders into position to remake the 5-point.

53. White 61: 13/19 3/2
Home free. Next job is to clear the 15-point. That won't be easy.

54. Black 53: 17/9

55. White 66: 18/24(2)
Forced play, but by giving up the 18-point, White has fewer rolls which clear the 15-point safely.

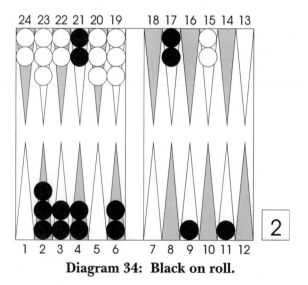

Diagram 34: **Black on roll.**

56. Black 11: 9/5
The fastest way to make a key point is to first slot it, then cover it later.

57. White 61: 15/22
Another forced play, and now here's a potential winning shot for
Black. He can hit with any two or six, or 11, 51, 15, or 33, a total
of 24 numbers out of 36. A hit isn't guaranteed to win, however,
because Black's 5-point is still open.

58. Black 31: 11/7
A key miss. Now the win is pretty much assured for White.
However, there's still some chance Black could be gammoned.

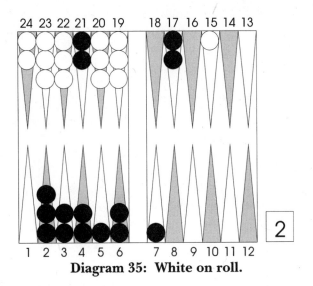

Diagram 35: White on roll.

59. White 53: 15/20 22/off
White actually has three ways to play this apparently simple roll.
Besides his actual play, he could try 15/20/23, bearing no men
off but leaving three men each on the 19-point and the 20-point,
or 15/20 19/22, leaving four men on the 20-point and just two
men on the 19-point. Which is best?

How To Bearoff
If White's only concern were safety, the right play would be 15/
20 19/22. In general, the safest way to bear off against contact
(Black's ownership of the 21-point creates contact as White tries
to clear the 19 and 20-points) is to strip down to two men on the

last point (the 19-point) as quickly as possible, then clear that point with a good throw.

Usually, however, safety is not the only issue. In this case, White also has to think about the possibility of winning or not winning a gammon. The best way to win a gammon is almost always to bear off checkers as fast as possible. That consideration argues for Magriel's actual play, 15/20 22/off.

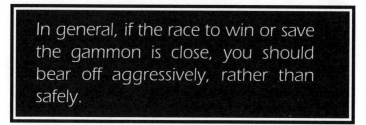

In general, if the race to win or save the gammon is close, you should bear off aggressively, rather than safely.

That's the case here. Good play by Magriel.

60. Black 64: 17/11 17/13

61. White 21: 23/off 24/off
As before, 19/22 was actually the safest play. But as before, Magriel's aggressive bearoff technique is correct. He's trying for a gammon to win the match, and he may get it.

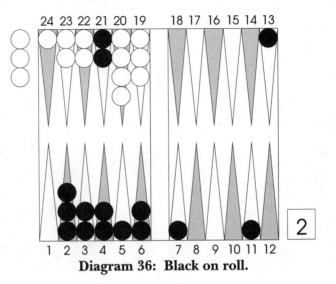

Diagram 36: Black on roll.

62. Black 61: 11/5 7/6
Black could play 13/6, wasting no pips in his race to save the gammon. Snelling's actual play wastes one pip, but it's correct since making the 5-point greatly enhances Black's winning chances in case he does hit a last-minute shot. (In this position, Black is about 8% to actually hit a shot as White tries to clear the 19 and 20-points.)

63. White 65: 19/off 20/off

64. Black 44: 21/5
This roll pretty much guarantees that Black will save the gammon.

65. White 63: 19/off 19/22

66. Black 41: 13/9 2/1

67. White 52: 20/off 23/off

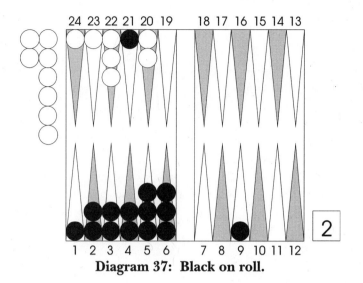

Diagram 37: **Black on roll.**

68. Black 43: 21/17 9/6
Black could stick around for another turn, hoping that White would throw 61, 51, or 41, which would give Black a chance to hit a winning shot. However, an unlucky sequence could then easily cost Black the gammon, so he's right to run.

69. White 44: 20/24(2) 22/off(2)

70. Black 64: 17/7

White wins a single game worth 2 points and takes a 10-9 lead.

Summary:
Pay close attention in this game to the interaction between match score and cube handling on the part of both players.

Snellings starts out with an early advantage. However, In a

position which he would easily double in a money game, he declines to turn the cube, since he has the possibility of winning the match with an undoubled gammon.

When the advantage suddenly shifts the other way, however, Magriel instantly doubles. He recognizes that giving the opponent a cube which can't be returned because of the match score entitles him to double quite aggressively.

Magriel goes on to win the game and take a 10-9 lead in the 11-point match. Had Snellings carelessly doubled (as many players would have done) he would have lost the entire match in this game.

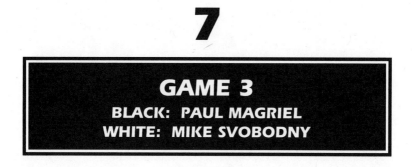

GAME 3
BLACK: PAUL MAGRIEL
WHITE: MIKE SVOBODNY

Mike Svobodny is the only player to have won both the World Championship in Monte Carlo (in 1984) and the World Cup (in 1992). He's one of the most feared pros on the international circuit.

This game was taken from a consolation match in the World Cup of 1988. At the time of this game, Magriel was leading 12-9 in a 25-point match.

1. White 62: 1/7 12/14
This is the standard opening play with a 62, splitting the back men to make an advanced anchor, while using the deuce to bring down a builder.

2. Black 21: 8/7* 13/11
Hitting with the ace is of course clear. With the deuce, it's slightly better to get another cover number for the blot than it is to split the back men.

3. White 62: Bar/2 1/7*
In and hit. White's opening play of a 62 has succeeded since he's now gained considerable ground in the race.

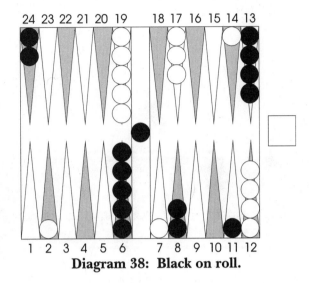

24 23 22 21 20 19   18 17 16 15 14 13

1   2   3   4   5   6   7   8   9   10 11 12

Diagram 38: Black on roll.

4. Black 21: Bar/23 8/7*

The first really difficult play of the game. Magriel's play, entering and hitting, is certainly reasonable, but it does leave two exposed blots and, more important, it breaks the 8-point.

> The 8-point is a key opening point, and as a rule you don't want to break it just to hit loose.

Two other good plays come to mind. One is Bar/24 13/11, which makes a new and potentially valuable point. The drawback here is that Black leaves three men on the 24-point, which is a weak and inflexible formation, usually to be avoided in the early game.

Put Your Checkers Where They Belong

The other try is Bar/23 6/5, which keeps the 8-point, diversifies the back checkers, and begins to unstack the 6-point. It's by far the prettiest play, but it does leave two blots vulnerable to threes and fours by White. However, the other plays all have drawbacks as well. Here's my rule for these situations:

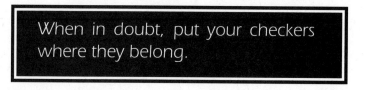

When in doubt, put your checkers where they belong.

The checkers on the 6-point should certainly be making the 5-point, so this play gets my vote.

5. White 32: Bar/2 12/15

I don't like this play. It's too early to make the 2-point, which can easily become a trap later on as Black starts to fill in a prime. Meantime, the 14-point is a nice point to own. I think a clearly better play was Bar/3 12/14.

Actually making points is better than preparing to make points.

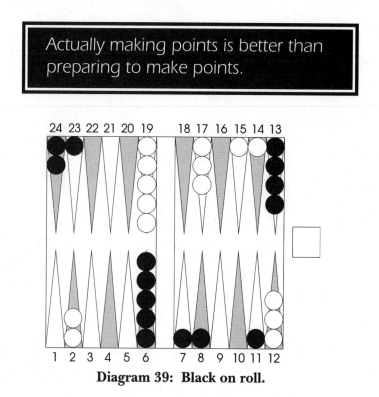

Diagram 39: Black on roll.

6. Black 51: 13/8 6/5

A bold and very ingenious play by Magriel! He remakes the valuable 8-point, then slots the key 5-point, leaving White a double shot: threes to hit on the 5-point and fives to hit on the 7-point. Although the play may look wild, the idea behind it is grounded in very solid logic.

- Note that White is very well placed to start building key points like the 20-point, 21-point, and 18-point. If White stops to hit one of Black's blots, he can't build his own key points.

- Black is already behind in the race, so falling a bit farther behind is not a big risk.

- If White doesn't hit either of these blots, Black will build a powerhouse position very quickly.

Having said this, we should note that Black had another reasonable, if unadventurous choice: the simple 8/7 23/18, building the 7-point while moving out to the opposing bar. Magriel's play, however, is characteristic of his uncompromising style.

7. White 31: 2/5* 2/3

One strength of Magriel's last play is that Svobodny is forced to hit with this roll rather than make the 20-point. I don't agree with the play of the ace, however. My preference is just to button up some of the blots with 14/15. The logic is this: For the next several turns, White and Black are going to be exchanging hits. It's quite unlikely that White will ever have a whole turn free to make use of the building potential of the blots on the 14 and 15-points. As a consequence, I would just consolidate now. White would still have a good, flexible position, but with less chance of an accident.

8. Black 31: Bar/22 6/5*

Right. With four men back, and White having no board and lots of building numbers, Black must hit and keep on hitting.

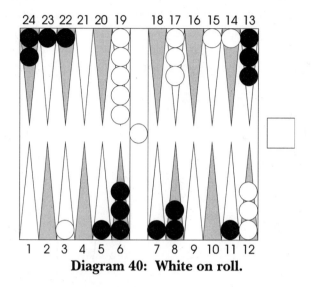

Diagram 40: White on roll.

9. White 55: Bar/5* 12/22* 17/22
A great shot! Svobodny rolls the first double and consolidates his advantage. Black may face a cube turn next roll.

10. Black 54: Bar/20 Bar/21

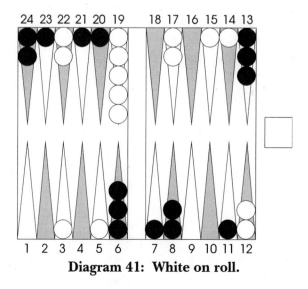

Diagram 41: White on roll.

White should double now. All of his rolls hit at least one checker and most rolls hit two checkers or make the 20 or 21-point on Black's head. Some of these sequences are utterly devastating, while almost all sequences leave White firmly in control. Black could get a good back game out of this position, but he might also end up with seven men trapped on the 24-point.

Doubling In The Opening

When you're looking to offer a double in the opening, you're generally looking for two criteria:

• A solid, clear advantage right now, coupled with ....

• The possibility of becoming a huge favorite in one turn.

Both those criteria are present here, and White should double.

11. White 32: 17/20* 19/21*

Excellent play by Svobodny. He hits on the two inner points to make it more difficult for Black to anchor. If Black fails to roll a four or a five, the game is over (White will double and Black must pass), while even if Black does roll a four or five he still won't have built an advanced anchor – he'll need at least one more roll for that.

12. Black 65: Bar/20*

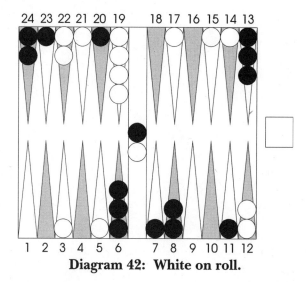

24 23 22 21 20 19   18 17 16 15 14 13

1 2 3 4 5 6   7 8 9 10 11 12

Diagram 42: White on roll.

White could think about doubling now, but his game is worse than it was a turn ago because he's on the bar.

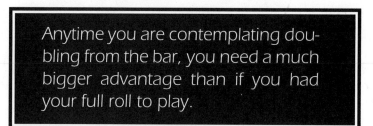

> Anytime you are contemplating doubling from the bar, you need a much bigger advantage than if you had your full roll to play.

13. White 64: Bar/4 14/20*
The same idea as with White's last play, and equally correct. Again, if Black fails to roll a four or a five, White will double and Black will pass.

14. Black 65: Bar/20*

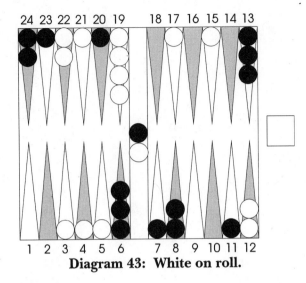

24 23 22 21 20 19   18 17 16 15 14 13

1 2 3 4 5 6   7 8 9 10 11 12

Diagram 43: White on roll.

Now White definitely doesn't have a double, as he's running out of ammunition to build his board.

15. White 43: Bar/4 17/20*

In backgammon, you have to be always alert to the slight changes in a position that signal a switch to a new strategy. On moves 11 and 13, I liked White's play of hitting and leaving blots on the 20 and 21-points. Now, though, it's time for White to change gears.

When To Change Plans

The super-aggressive plan he pursued before was justified when White had plenty of outfield builders, ready to cover the blots if they weren't hit. With four of his own men sent back, however, White needs to realize that a long game is in order and a quick knockout is no longer possible. The right idea now is to consolidate with Bar/3 17/21.

> Backgammon can't be played with blinders on. Every move creates a new situation, potentially calling for a change of plan.

16. Black 11: Bar/24 Bar/23 6/5*

Great shot by Magriel! With Black's back game firmly in place, White won't be thinking about doubling for some time now. Hitting with the ace is correct since it cuts down on White's chances of making the 20 or 21-points.

17. White 63: Bar/3 15/21

Essentially forced. White at least emerges from the fireworks with a three-point board.

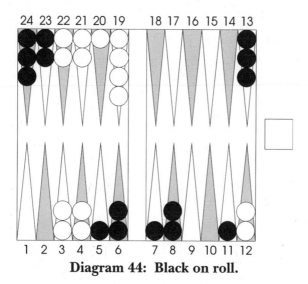

Diagram 44: Black on roll.

18. Black 65: 13/7 11/6

Black has several choices with this roll, but Magriel finds the best play.

Duplication

By making the 7-point and posting a builder on the 6, he duplicates White's aces (White needs aces to hit on the 5-point and make the 20-point), cutting down on White's total of effective numbers. If he had chosen instead to play 11/5 13/8, White would need aces to cover the 20, and different numbers (threes and fours) to hit on the 7-point.

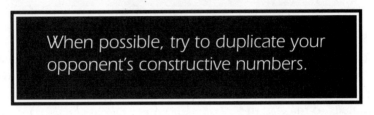

When possible, try to duplicate your opponent's constructive numbers.

Another play was 24/18 23/18, but this would have been bad on several counts. Not only does it fail to build a **front position** (the 5-point through the 8-point are Black's front position) but by giving up one of the two back-game anchors, it raises the specter that White may resume his attack.

19. White 53: 12/20

Nice roll and well-played. White has a solid edge now, with Black's men trapped further back than White's men.

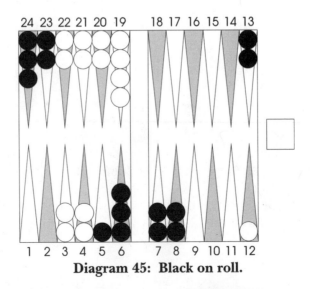

Diagram 45: Black on roll.

20. Black 31: 13/10 6/5

Another excellent play by Magriel. He could hit the blot on the 12-point, but with four White men already trapped, making the key 5-point is far more important.

> If you have several enemy men already in your home board, it's more important to strengthen your prime than to send still more men back.

Black is playing what's called a two-way game here. If White throws an awkward number, say 44 or 33 or 43, Black may be able to win by keeping White's men trapped. On the other hand, if White pops out and hits the blots, Black may be able to build a well-timed 1-2 back game with good winning chances later. It's a fun, flexible strategy which leads to interesting games and good winning chances.

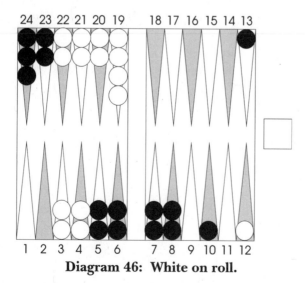

Diagram 46: White on roll.

21. White doubles to 2.

A pretty reasonable double according to the principles we discussed after Black's 10th move. White has an edge, since his prime is farther advanced than Black's. In addition, he has lots of possibilities of increasing his advantage this turn. All his sixes and ones hit, and he can also hit with 54 for good measure. A hit here will pretty much end Black's chances of winning going forward, that is, by trapping White behind a better prime.

Although hitting will push Black into a back game, it's not clear how strong that back game will be. Black might develop good timing, or he might not. All in all, a good double.

22. Black takes.

Sure. White hits with 22 numbers, but he misses with 14, and Black is certainly doing well in that case. He also has chances to develop a well-timed ace-deuce back game, while the game could take other directions as well. There's much too much play left to give this one up.

23. White 31: 12/13* 19/22

A pretty good result. Hitting with a six was better, since it also released a back man, but White will settle for this number.

24. Black stays out.

It's looking like Black may be forced into a back game.

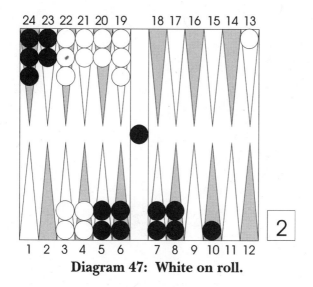

24 23 22 21 20 19   18 17 16 15 14 13

1 2 3 4 5 6   7 8 9 10 11 12

Diagram 47: White on roll.

25. White 11: 3/4 19/21 13/14
A good roll but an odd play. There's no advantage to leaving a checker back on the 3-point. White should play two men from the 3-point to the 4-point, ready to hop over Black's prime with fives and sixes, then move the other two aces from 13 to 15. This is what we call a **nullo play** – a play with no possible upside.

26. Black 51: Bar/24 10/5
Black needs both anchors to play a back game, so jumping out with 23/18 is a very bad play.

27. White 55: 4/9(3) 9/14
Ironic – the misplay of the ace last turn may actually be important.

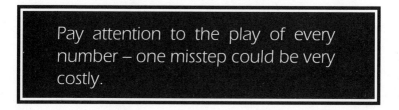

Pay attention to the play of every number – one misstep could be very costly.

94

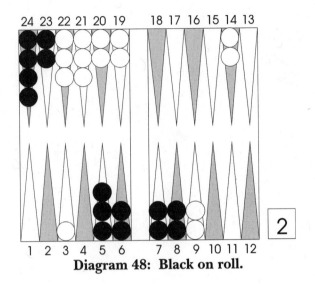

Diagram 48: Black on roll.

28. Black 51: 24/18

Very good. Black escapes a checker, which helps his timing and outfield control, while preserving both back game points.

29. White 53: 9/14 9/12

This play is pretty much forced, and it has the merit of duplicating sixes.

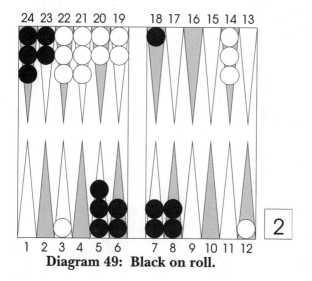

Diagram 49: Black on roll.

30. Black 42: 18/12*

This puts a second checker behind a four-prime, which might actually hold up in this position. Breaking the prime to make the 3-point (7/3* 5/3) is much more problematical. It commits Black to a forward-attacking strategy as the alternative to his back game, but if the attacking game fails, the back game timing is likely to be much worse. This is a key concept.

> If you're committed to winning in a back game, don't be in a hurry to make inner board points.

31. White 54: Bar/4/9

A clear play. White needs to escape whenever he can.

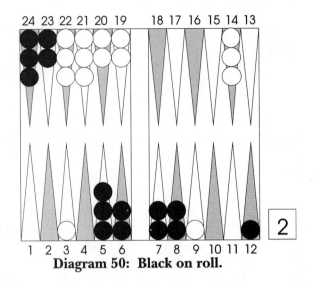

Diagram 50: Black on roll.

32. Black 65: 24/18 12/7

A smooth play. Black also has to get spare checkers into the outfield whenever possible, so 24/18 seems clear. Leaving the checker on the 18-point gives good outfield coverage, so if White doesn't hit with a four, he may have to leave an awkward shot.

Playing 24/13 doesn't really leave White any bad rolls. If White doesn't hit the blots on the 12 and 13 points, he will either move from the 3 to the 9-point, or just move the checker on the 9-point to safety.

A somewhat different plan is to make the 18-point with 24/18 23/18. However, this opens up the possibility that White will make the 23-point himself, leaving Black with just the 18-point and the 24-point. This is well-known to be a very weak defensive formation, little better than just the 24-point by itself.

Magriel's actual play looks clearly best.

33. White 52: 14/19 9/11

White has to leave a loose checker somewhere in the outfield, so he minimizes Black's hitting possibilities by leaving a blot seven pips away from the 18-point.

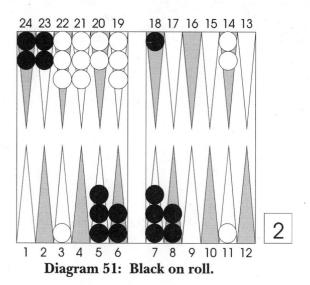

Diagram 51: Black on roll.

34. Black 32: 18/13

A reasonable play, moving in the outfield while keeping his prime intact.

Back Game Strategy

Another, and completely different idea, was the daring 7/4 5/ 3*! This move can work in two ways. If White replies with a poor shot like 51 or 61, his back checker could get stuck behind Black's prime. If White hits both blots, Black's back game timing could improve.

Remember, if you're playing a back game, and your checkers aren't completely trapped, you may be better off having more checkers hit, since you may be able to hold your position longer.

On the other hand, it's not at all clear that Magriel needs to make such a wide-open play. White may have difficulty extricating his checker after normal moves, so I prefer Magriel's actual play. However, if you're going to play back games, you need to be aware of the possibility of plays like 7/4 and 5/3*. Under the right circumstances, they may be clearly correct.

35. White 64: 3/13*
White hops out (finally) and hits. A good shot.

36. Black 62: Bar/23/17
Clear-cut. Black escapes for more timing. Notice how Black is able to preserve his position by being hit, reentering, and moving into the outfield.

This technique is called recirculating checkers, and it's fundamental to a well-played back game.

37. White 66: 11/17* 13/19 14/20(2)
A completely forced play. However, strategically this is a bad roll for White. White's men are essentially home, and Black's timing

is still in fine shape. Black will be able to wait for a winning shot while he builds his home board, and he shouldn't be in any danger of moving his men to the low points in his board prematurely.

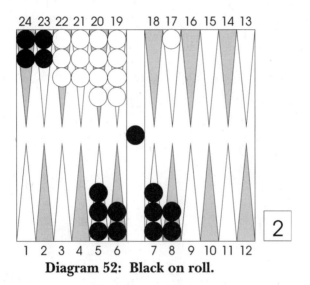

Diagram 52: Black on roll.

38. Black 21: Bar/23 5/4

Correct. As we've seen in our previous two games, Black's proper strategy is to slot the next point of his prime (in this case the 4-point) then cover the next turn, while preparing to slot again. He'll do this until he has made the strongest possible home board.

39. White 43: 17/21 19/22

The safest way to bear off is to quickly strip down to two checkers on the rearmost point, then clear that point on the next roll. By that rule, this is the safest way for White to play 43.

40. Black 22: 8/4 7/3

Black covers, then slots the next point of the prime. That's the ideal way to build up the board.

41. White 52: 20/off 19/21
Taking off a checker with the five is forced; with the two, White prepares to clear the 19-point next turn.

42. Black 61: 23/16
This roll isn't useful for extending the prime, so Black springs another checker into the outfield.

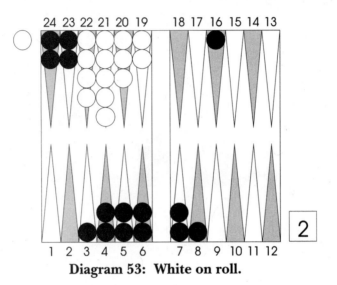

Diagram 53: White on roll.

43. White 31: 19/22 19/20
Correct. White clears the rearmost point. A very good roll. His next job is to clear the 20-point.

44. Black 54: 16/12 8/3
With the five, Black covers his slotted point, giving him a very strong 5-point prime. It will be very difficult for White to escape Black's blockade, should he get hit later. With the four, Black brings up the next builder.

45. White 22: 20/22(4)
Forced, of course, but also an excellent shot, clearing the 20-point. White now has plenty of spares and only two points to clear.

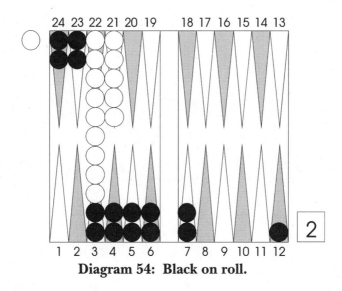

Diagram 54: Black on roll.

46. Black 63: 23/14

Creating Shots

An excellent play by Magriel. If we look at White's position, notice that White can play almost all his numbers safely. Threes, fours, fives, and sixes bear off checkers, while aces can be played from the 21-point to the 22-point. The only other number, deuces, can't be played at all. By moving off the 23-point, Magriel gives White a way to play a two – from 21 to 23, leaving a blot!

> Remember this motif – it's a key idea in defending many positions. Always check to see how your opponent's numbers actually play.

47. White 65: 21/off(2)

48. Black 22: 12/10 14/8
Black's next goal is to extend his 5-point prime into a full 6-point prime.

> Usually, the easiest way to extend a prime is to slot the back of the prime.

That's especially true if a shot is coming soon. Black slots the back of the prime and prepares to cover with a deuce.

49. White 66: 21/off(3) 22/off
Another great shot by White. Now he has only one point left to clear.

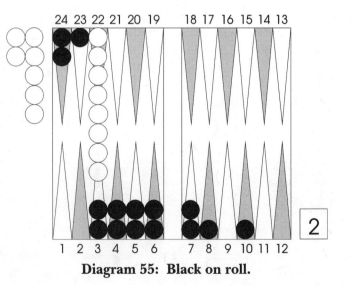

Diagram 55: Black on roll.

50. Black 53: 10/2

Black has a bunch of plays here. The key decision he has to make is this: What's the right arrangement of his three back checkers that generates the most chance of hitting White?

Here are his four plays:

• He could run with two men, 23/18 and 24/21. This minimizes the chances that Black will get backgammoned, while guaranteeing a shot if White rolls an ace or a deuce. However, in this variation Black gets only one shot. If White, for example, leaves a shot by rolling a deuce and Black misses it, Black will enter high in the board and lose any later shot vigorish. This is by far the weakest play.

• He could run from the back point with 24/16. This gives a single shot next turn if White rolls a deuce, and a double shot if White rolls an ace. However, the two loose blots are much more vulnerable now that Black has lost the security of a solid point. The rolls of 11 and 22 are real crushers for White, while 21, which White would play 3/1*/off, is also good. This play is too risky.

• Running off the front point with 23/15 is a little better. Although Black can't get any double shots in this variation, he will get a single shot if White rolls an ace, and this shot will repeat if White doesn't then roll a second ace. This isn't a bad play.

• Best of all is to leave all the checkers where they are and just play 10/2. He gets a double shot if White rolls an ace, and preserves the option of splitting off the 24-point later. Also, he preserves his later chances of getting a shot if White rolls 21 or 22.

Excellent play by Magriel.

51. White 51: 22/off 22/23*
Finally! Now Black has a chance to turn the game around by hitting this shot.

52. Black 52: Bar/23* 7/2
And he does! With his very best number, in fact. Black hits and simultaneously covers the deuce-point.

53. White stays out.

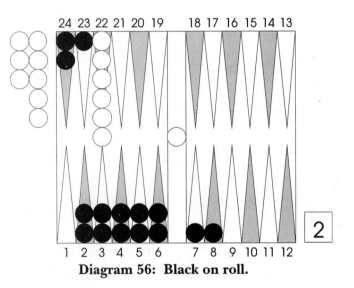

Diagram 56: Black on roll.

54. Black doubles to 4.
An interesting double my Magriel. He's certainly become a favorite in the game, but is it time to turn the cube? Let's take a look at how this position is likely to develop.

The most likely probability is that Magriel will complete his 6-point prime and eventually close out White's checker, but without hitting a second checker. In this case, with White already having eight men off, Black will be a slight favorite, probably in the neighborhood of 60% to win. (If White had borne off nine checkers before being hit, then he would still be the favorite. These are good facts to remember.)

If White exposes a second checker, and Black hits it, and Black then closes out both checkers, he will be a huge favorite – actually considerably more than 90% to win.

There are a few other odd variations. Black might never complete his prime, and White might enter and escape. That's obviously very bad for Black. Or Black might hit a second checker but White might anchor both checkers on the 1-point. Black's about 75% to win if that happens.

Doubling After A Back Game

So – should Black double or not? The answer is that it's still a little premature to turn the cube. Although Black is a favorite in almost all variations, there's nothing happening in the position that will make Black a huge favorite. Remember our discussion of doubling in the previous two games. In order to offer a good double, it's not enough to just be a favorite in the position – you also have to have a threat which, if carried out on the next turn, will make you such a big favorite that White would have to pass your double. Nothing like that is happening yet in this position. White has an easy take, and he'll have an easy take next turn in almost every case.

> Here's a good rule for doubling in unclear positions: When in doubt, don't double. When you're not sure that doubling is correct, hold onto the cube. It's a very valuable asset.

55. White takes.
A very clear take on White's part, although he's now an underdog in the game. His chances won't dip below 25% until Black hits a second checker, and that's a ways off.

56. Black 53: 23/15

As long as White is on the bar, Black's strategy is straightforward. (As we say in backgammon, "A matter of technique.") His first goal is to complete a 6-point prime so that White's checker will not be able to escape. To do this, Black will leave the checker slotted on the 7-point, and prepare to cover it.

Right now he has ones to cover from the 8-point. By moving to the 15-point, he also gives himself eights to cover. Next turn, he'll move the checker on the 15-point to within direct range of the 7-point (someplace where a single number on a die could cover), and then start his other checkers moving.

The faint of heart might now inquire, "Isn't Black risking a loss if White rolls a 16 from the bar?" The answer is, not really. First of all, 16 is a great shot whether Black has a checker on the 7 or not. Second, even if White rolls the 16, Black will have plenty of chances to hit the checker as it tries to come around the board. And finally, the long-run danger that would result from never making a 6-point prime outweighs the short-run risk of a 16.

Plays that masters make routinely, like leaving the bar slotted in this position, look bold to the uninitiated. Once you understand the reasons behind the play, however, it's not bold at all, simply logical.

57. White stays out.

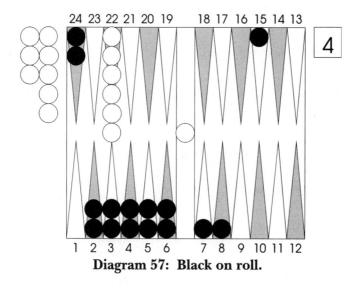

Diagram 57: Black on roll.

58. Black 31: 8/7 15/12
Mission accomplished. Black has a full prime, so White cannot escape once he enters. Black's next job is to bring a spare checker into position to slot the ace-point.

59. White stays out.

60. Black 51: 12/7 24/23
From the 7-point, Black can move the spare to the ace-point with any 6. Now he starts the next back checker moving.

61. White stays out.
By the way, White is quite happy to stay on the bar for as long as possible! Why? He has nothing to gain by entering now, since he can't escape. But if he does enter, he might then throw an ace or a deuce, exposing a new checker to a hit.

As we saw before, Black can only become a big favorite in this position by hitting, then closing out, a second checker. If White sits on the bar long enough, Black will eventually be forced to close his ace-point, and that variation will then never occur.

62. Black 43: 23/16
Black comes closer.

63. White stays out.

64. Black 44: 16/4 7/3
Black should be able to slot and eventually close his ace-point without difficulty, but numbers like 44 and 55 can spell trouble. Black's checkers could be forced into a position they don't really want to be in. No real danger yet, though.

65. White stays out.

66. Black 61: 24/17
Black wanted to roll a three or a two, to slot the ace-point, but he still has plenty of time.

67. White stays out.

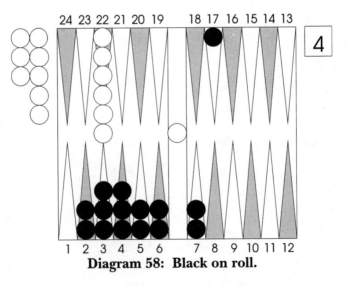

Diagram 58: Black on roll.

68. Black 31: 4/1 17/16
Finally Black gets to slot.

69. White stays out.

White has stayed out for eight consecutive turns! That's very unlikely. The odds of that occurring are about 17-1 against, as a matter of fact. However, it's been a very lucky break for White. He's never had to expose a second checker, and Black's men are almost all the way home.

70. Black 54: 16/7

This is almost Black's worst roll. He can't cover the one-point, and he can't even get a new number to cover. If he can't roll a six or a two next turn, he may have to break his prime without ever closing his board.

71. White stays out.

Nine dances in a row!

72. Black 43: 7/4 7/3

An amazing sequence. Black has been forced to break his carefully constructed 6-point prime. Now White really does want to roll an ace!

73. White stays out.

Oops. Ten dances in a row.

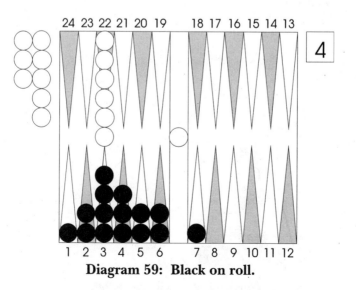

Diagram 59: Black on roll.

74. Black 32: 7/5 4/1

Black finally covers the ace-point, but makes a slight technical error in doing so. Better was 7/4 3/1, leaving Black with an even number of checkers on the two high points. After Black's actual play, the rolls of 66 and 55, which should be his best shots, actually leave a blot on the 5-point.

Bearing Off Strategy

> In most situations in the bearoff, it's right to leave yourself with an even number of checkers on your two highest points.

75. White can't move.

76. Black 32: 5/off

77. White can't move.

78. Black 62: 6/off 6/4

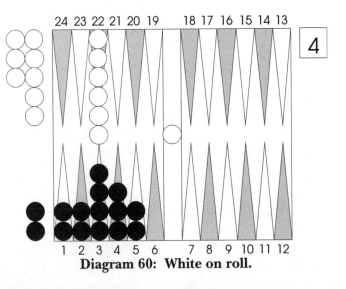

Diagram 60: White on roll.

79. White 63: Bar/9

After a long time on the bar, White finally enters. To bear off, White will have to cross two quadrants to get this checker into the home board, then bear off seven checkers. That's a total of nine crossovers. (A **crossover** is just a move of a checker from one quadrant to another, or off the board. Counting crossovers is a quick way of getting an estimate of who's ahead in the race.) Black, meanwhile, is on roll needing 13 crossovers.

It looks like White is ahead, but remember that Black is pretty much guaranteed to bear off two checkers each turn, while if White rolls small numbers, he may fail to get a crossover.

80. Black 53: 5/off 3/off

A good roll, taking men off the highest points.

81. White 33: 9/21

Excellent! White should be able to redouble next turn.

82. Black 63: 5/off 3/off

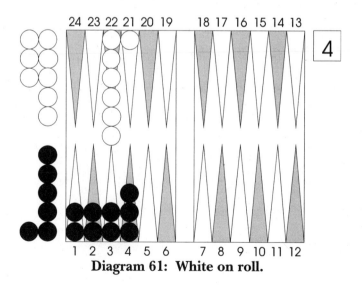

Diagram 61: White on roll.

A very clear redouble. White has seven men left, Black has nine. White also leads in the pip count, 22 to 24.

> If both sides are bearing off, and you have both fewer checkers and fewer pips, you are almost guaranteed to have a strong double.

84. Black takes.

No. This is a clear pass. In general, if you trail in the pip count, you need fewer checkers than your opponent in order to take. This is even more true when most checkers are off the board, as here. Black will actually win this position less than 20% of the time, not the 25% he needs to take a double.

Even though Black rolls a large double in the bearoff and White doesn't, Black still loses the game, a sure sign of an incorrect take.

85. White 22: 21/off 22/24(2)

86. Black 55: 4/off(3) 3/off

87. White 41: 22/off 24/off

88. Black 43: 3/off 2/off

89. White 65: 22/off(2)

90. Black 65: 2/off 1/off

White wins 8 points.

Summary:

The game begins with an all-out struggle for control of key points, characteristic of modern backgammon at its best. Svobodny jumps out to an early lead, but misses a chance to give a good double on move 11. Over the next few moves Magriel's position improves as he builds a block of his own.

Finally Svobodny gets to offer another good double as Magriel is forced to expose a couple of blots. A quick hit leads to Magriel's playing a classic, well-timed 1-2 back game.

Magriel shows good defensive technique in opening the 2-point at just the right time. His good technique pays off as Svobodny leaves a shot and gets hit. Magriel quickly redoubles and completes a full prime, but Svobodny stays on the bar and thwarts Magriel's plan to catch a second checker.

Svobodny eventually enters from the bar as soon as Magriel opens his board, and gets around quickly enough to win by one roll.

8

Joe Sylvester has been one of the world's top-10 players for the past dozen years. He burst onto the backgammon scene by winning the World Amateur Championship in 1983. He has since won many American tournaments including the Reno tournament from which this game is taken. He has an especially fine record in the World Cup, winning World Cup I in 1988 and finishing second in World Cup IV in 1994.

This game was played in the finals of the Reno Master's tournament of 1992. Sylvester was leading 5-1 in the 25-point match, which he eventually won, 25-22.

1. White 43: 12/16 12/15
In top-flight backgammon today, there are several popular ways of playing an opening 43, each with its own adherents. The idea of Snelling's play is to bring down builders to make the key 20-point, 21-point, and 18-point. To achieve this building potential, White has to take certain risks. His blots on the 16 and 15-points are exposed to hits if Black throws any eight or nine. All told, Black will be able to hit a blot about one time in three.

Two other plays try to achieve a balance between building and splitting, with a bit less risk. The play which has been most popular for the past 15 years or so is 1/5 12/15. The checker on the 15-point gives White some new point-making numbers, like 62, 51, and 63, while the split to the 5-point prepares to make the most valuable anchor. The checker on the 15-point is only exposed to nines, so White is less likely to fall behind in the race after this play.

Splitting In The Opening

A new play, which has been gaining popularity in the last few years, is 1/4 12/16. For building purposes, the checker on the 16-point is actually a little more valuable than a checker on the 15-point, as it generates more new point-making combinations.

The idea of splitting to the 4-point rather than the 5-point is part of a new theory of splitting: *Don't split to the point that your opponent MOST wants to make, if you have a choice.* The point that Black most wants to make in this position is his 5-point. If you split there, and he points on you, he's accomplished two objectives at once – putting you on the bar, and making the best point in his board.

By splitting to the 4-point instead, Black can at most accomplish one objective. He can point on you, or make his best point, but not both at once.

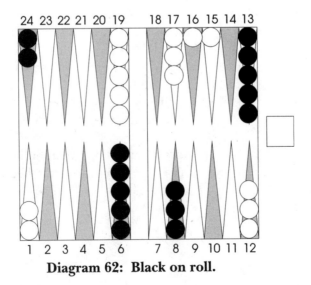

Diagram 62: Black on roll.

2. Black 53: 24/16*
Black could also make his 3-point with this roll, but he chooses to hit instead. That's right.

> Given a choice between hitting a blot on the other side of the board and making an inner point, you should generally hit.

Hitting accomplishes two good things: you gain ground in the race, and you escape one of your back checkers. Making a point accomplishes only one good thing. Two good things are better than one good thing.

3. White 51: Bar/5 15/16*
Entering and hitting is clear. The game is still about even.

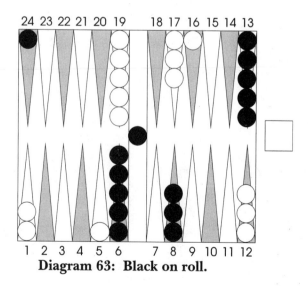

Diagram 63: Black on roll.

4. Black 54: Bar/16*
Black hits, although there's another good play: Bar/20 24/20. (Making the 20-point in this way is known as "A Barabino", in honor of Rick Barabino, who has rolled this number in many game-saving situations.) Hitting here is right, however, for the same reason as in the comment to move 2.

5. White stays out.
White rolls 66 and stays on the bar. A bad break, as that was the only number that wouldn't let him enter. One reason that hitting is so powerful in the early game is that these disaster shots are always lurking around when you're on the bar.

6. Black 21: 6/5* 13/11
Simple and very strong. Sylvester unstacks his two big points, puts a second White checker on the bar, and prepares to build the 5-point. It's hard to do more with a single roll.

7. White 62: Bar/2

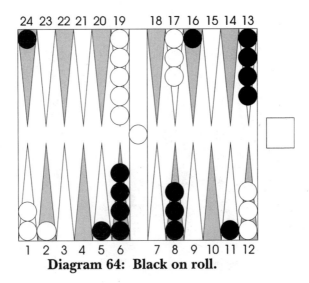

Diagram 64: Black on roll.

8. Black doubles to 2.

A strong double. Black is ahead in all key phases of the game. He has a big lead in the race (156 pips to 189), he has escaped a checker while White has four men back, and he has plenty of builders in position to work on his prime. Making the 5-point is virtually a sure thing, and the bar or the 4-point should follow soon. A fine double by Sylvester.

9. White takes.

Just because Black has a double doesn't mean White should drop. Next turn White will likely face just a two point board. That means White should have no trouble entering and starting his own development. White could create a high anchor game, a massive back game, or a counter-prime of his own. He's certainly an underdog, but there's a ton of play left. Good take by Snellings.

10. Black 55: 16/11 13/3 8/3

A constructive shot, although it's one of the few numbers that doesn't make the 5-point. Black makes the 3-point and the 11-point, and prepares for more progress next turn.

11. White stays out.

Dancing now was much more serious than dancing two turns ago. That dance just gave Black a healthy initiative; this turn on the bar may give Black the time to pin White into an ace-point game.

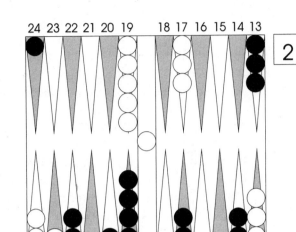

Diagram 65: Black on roll.

12. Black 43: 8/5 6/2*

Sylvester correctly goes for the throat. *His goal now is to prevent White from establishing a second anchor in the home board.* That second anchor would give White a full-fledged back game, with winning chances in the 35% to 50% range, depending on how well-timed the back game turned out to be. If Black can capture the 2-point and force White to play just a pure ace-point game, White's winning chances will be in the 20% to 30% range. That's a big improvement for Black, and it certainly justifies attacking on the 2-point until Black runs out of ammunition.

13. White 32: Bar/2*

White's moves will be forced for some time. Here he can only enter one checker from the bar.

14. Black 42: Bar/23 6/2*

As we indicated before, Black will attack on the 2-point until someone makes that point, after which the battle will shift to other fronts. It's often the case that a point becomes so valuable that both players throw all their energies into an all-out struggle to make the key point. Games which hinge on struggles for key points are usually the most complex and demanding.

15. White 64: Bar/4

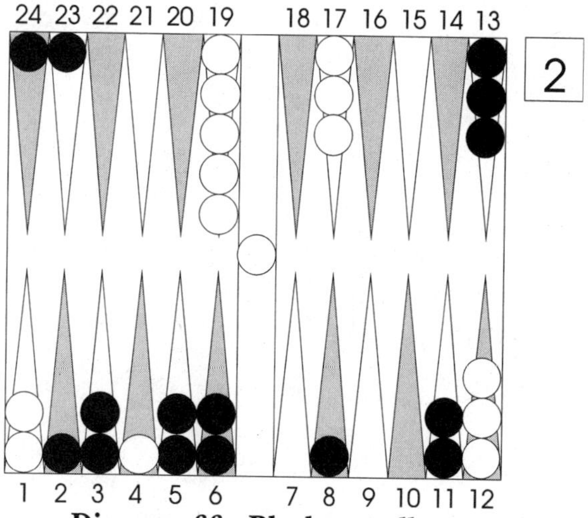

Diagram 66: Black on roll.

16. Black 64: 8/2 11/7

First mission accomplished: Black has made the 2-point. Now a new struggle develops over the 4-point. If White can make the 4-point, he'll have what's called a 1-4 back game. That's not one of the stronger back games, but it will still be far more dangerous than a simple ace-point game.

Using Checkers Efficiently

The checker Black placed on the 7-point is a builder for the 4-point, but it's also a slot for the 7 itself. If White makes the 4-point, the 7-point will be the next battleground. Playing 11/7 has accomplished two objectives with one play, as opposed to a play like 13/9, which only provides a builder for the 4-point. Top players know how to use their checkers efficiently, and this play is a good example.

17. White stays out.

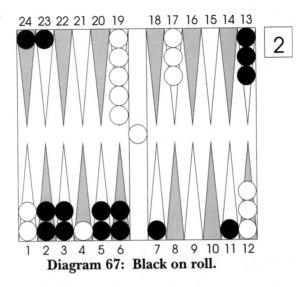

24 23 22 21 20 19   18 17 16 15 14 13

2

1 2 3 4 5 6   7 8 9 10 11 12

Diagram 67: Black on roll.

18. Black 32: 7/4* 11/9

Hits on the 4-point, and brings a number within direct range to cover. There was another reasonable way to accomplish the same objective: 7/4* 6/4, after which the checker on the 11-point would be a cover for the blot on the 6-point. The plays are about equally good.

19. White stays out.

20. Black 65: 9/4 13/7

Black has won the fight for the 4-point, and now slots the last point he needs to make; the 7-point. Once he makes that, White's checkers will be locked in behind six points in a row, and Black can then start moving his back men around.

21. White stays out.

22. Black 32: 23/21 13/10

Playing 13/10 provides two cover numbers for the 7-point (sixes and threes). Black can't do better than that, so he gets the back checkers moving with the deuce.

23. White stays out.

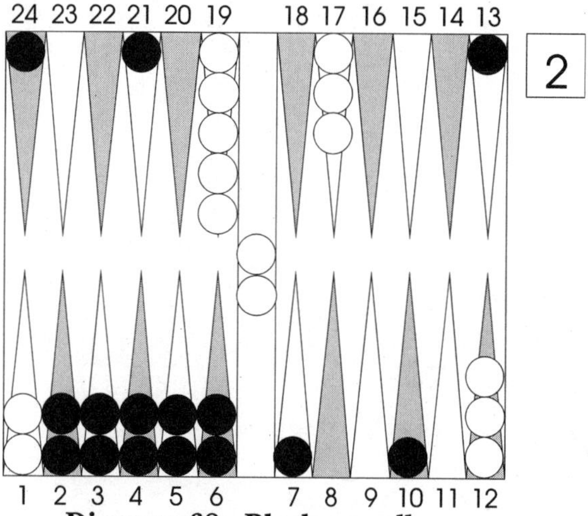

Diagram 68: Black on roll.

24. Black 31: 10/7 21/20
Black completes his 6-prime with the three and continues moving in back.

25. White stays out.

26. Black 61: 20/13
This escapes one back checker.

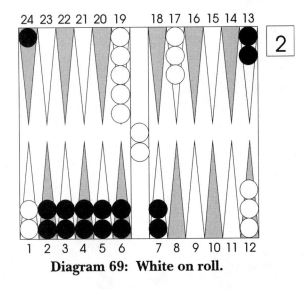

Diagram 69: White on roll.

27. White 11: Bar/1(2) 19/20(2)

A great shot, and suddenly it's a much more interesting middlegame. Although Black is still favored to get his back checker to safety eventually, White is back in the game and can start building a prime of his own.

28. Black 41: 13/9 24/23

Here's an example of how things can get awkward quickly. Black of course will keep his 6-prime as long as possible. Note that since the prime keeps four of White's checkers penned in, White only has 11 checkers left to play with, not enough to complete a prime of his own, even with optimal placement.

Since Black won't move the 12 checkers that make his prime, he has to play the four from the midpoint, leaving a blot there. It will be costly for him if this blot gets hit; he'll then have to escape two checkers from behind White's position, while only having the spare on the 9-point to move in case of an awkward number.

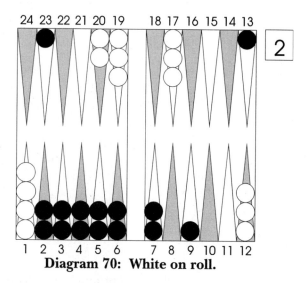

Diagram 70: White on roll.

29. White 32: 12/15 19/21

An excellent play by Snellings. He has several safe plays available to him. He could try the simple 12/17, or 12/15 17/19, or 12/14 17/20. All of these play marginally increase his building opportunities at the cost of, at most, a couple of indirect shots. Why did he instead choose to leave a direct shot on the 21-point at a time when Black's board is so strong?

Building A Prime Quickly

Part of the answer is contained in my comment to a previous play. White just doesn't have very many checkers left to build a prime of his own. With four checkers already trapped, he only has 11 checkers left. That's just enough to build five points with a spare left over. In order to build a prime, White's going to have to use his checkers very efficiently. The most efficient way to use your checkers is to put them right on the points you want to make.

White's second problem is time. Black has only one checker to escape. Pretty soon he's going to throw a number which will get him out of White's home board. For a prime to be useful, White will have to build it very quickly. That also argues for slotting and covering; White just doesn't have the luxury of waiting around to throw perfect numbers.

The last factor to be considered is the downside of slotting. What happens if White slots but gets hit? The downside, of course, is that White's more likely to get gammoned in that case. But notice that with four men already back, White is likely to get gammoned anyway if he loses this game. The best way for White to avoid being gammoned is to win the game, and the best play for that is Snelling's play, 19/21 and 12/15.

Alert, first-rate play by Snellings.

30. Black 51: 13/8 23/22

Playing to the 8-point gets one checker out of danger, while moving up to the 22-point gives two numbers to escape (sixes and fours) rather than just one (fives).

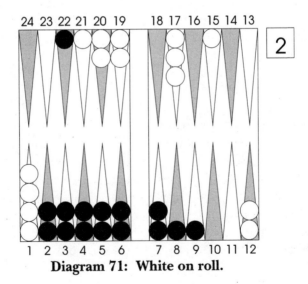

Diagram 71: White on roll.

31. White 31: 15/18 17/18

This unassuming little move is an incredibly great play, in fact probably the most difficult play to find in all the games in this book! Last turn White, at some risk, slotted the 21-point. Now he rolls a number that not only covers the 21-point but does so while leaving a good distribution of builders. Playing 17/21 seems so obvious that 9 out of 10 top players would make the move in a flash. Yet Snellings refuses to cover the blot, and instead leaves it exposed while making a different blocking point. What's going on?

Making The Right Points

The slight problem with making the 21-point is that it isn't really an effective blocking point. After 17/21, Black can leap into the outfield with all fours and sixes, after which White will have to hit or else revert to a straight ace-point game.

Making the 18-point, on the other hand, forms a much better blockade. Now Black only has sixes to leap, while his other big numbers (fives, fours, and threes) are stopped. If Black has to play those numbers on his side of the board, he'll have to give up the 7-point pretty soon. In fact, Black really has only one spare turn. A roll of 54, for instance, forces Black to move the checkers on his 8 and 9-points into his board. Next turn, fives and fours will make him break his 7-point.

What Snellings saw was that it's so hugely important for him to break Black's 7-point that it's worth taking the extra chance of being hit. Once the 7-point goes, White can move back into the outfield with some of those checkers on the 1-point, and the timing of the game will once again favor him.

A very difficult play to find, and a marvelous example of Snelling's talent for the game.

32. Black 53: 9/6 8/3
The plan starts to pay off as Black is now stripped of builders.

33. White 42: 12/18
White keeps his blockade in place and prepares to make the 21-point.

34. Black 55: 7/2(2)
There goes the 7-point! Now any six leaves White in excellent shape.

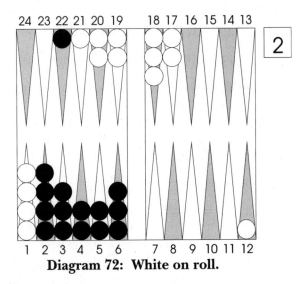

Diagram 72: White on roll.

35. White 33: 12/21 18/21
Not a six, but White is able to make five points in a row. Notice how efficiently he has used his checkers since he entered from the bar.

36. Black 51: 6/5 No 5.
Since Black can't play fives, this isn't such a bad roll. He preserves his position for another roll while waiting for a six.

37. White 63: 1/10
A great shot, keeping his prime while covering the outfield.

38. Black 62: 22/14
Running for home.

39. White 31: 10/14*
Halt! Black goes back behind the prime.

40. Black stays out.

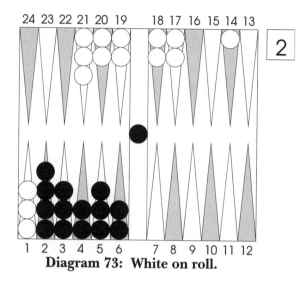

Diagram 73: White on roll.

41. White 44: 18/22(2) 14/22

White's last two rolls were very good, but this shot gobbles up most of his remaining timing. There was no way to preserve five consecutive points, so White starts to fill in his board.

42. Black stays out.

Dancing is actually not so bad for Black, since every roll he stays on the bar keeps his prime from breaking. This is a typical situation in prime against prime battles.

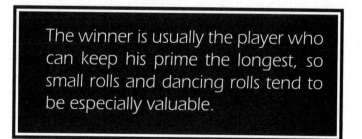

The winner is usually the player who can keep his prime the longest, so small rolls and dancing rolls tend to be especially valuable.

43. White 53: 17/22 17/20
White's timing is getting critical. Now he needs a six very soon.

44. Black stays out.

45. White 43: 20/24 21/24
Just small enough to keep his board intact!

46. Black stays out.

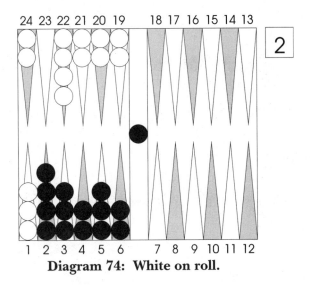

Diagram 74: White on roll.

47. White 11: 22/23(2) 19/20(2)
After four turns without a six, White's position finally cracks.

Killing Numbers
Fortunately for him, this rolls cracks in the least destructive way.
White keeps a five pointboard, and by breaking the 6-point,
White kills fives. On subsequent turns, White will hop with sixes,
but he won't have to play fives since he has no checkers left on
his 6-point. This has the effect of preserving his prime longer.

> In prime against prime struggles, look
> for ways to kill particular numbers.
> This will enable you to hold your
> prime as long as possible.

48. Black stays out.

49. White 52: 20/22
White's idea pays off as he only has to move two pips.

50. Black stays out.

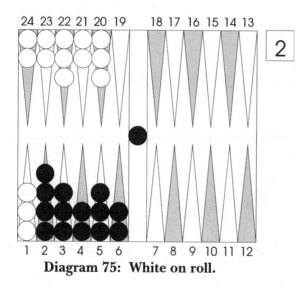

Diagram 75: White on roll.

51. White 65: 1/12
Excellent. The checker on the 12-point will buy White a few
more turns, helping him keep what's left of his prime.

52. Black stays out.

53. White 61: 1/8
Another great shot! One more six and White will be the favorite.

54. Black stays out.

55. White 51: 8/13 12/13
Making this point has the advantage of blocking a 66 by Black, which would otherwise be a winning number.

56. Black 65: Bar/14
After eight turns on the bar, Black finally enters. White needs an ace or a six, else Black will be in control again.

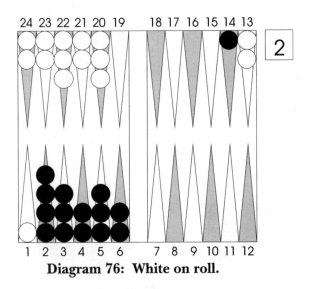

Diagram 76: White on roll.

57. White 51: 13/14* 13/18
White has a choice with this play. After hitting, he could keep the checker going and slot the 19-point with 13/14*/19. In some situations, this sort of play is correct, particularly if White could turn the cube after Black dances. That's not the case here. Since White still has to escape one more checker from behind Black's prime, White couldn't consider doubling in that case.

Snelling's more conservative play is clearly correct, even though White probably won't ever make the 19-point.

58. Black stays out.

59. White 51: 14/19 18/19
But the dice always have surprises in store! White rolls his best number, closing the board and now he's a clear favorite.

60. Black can't play.

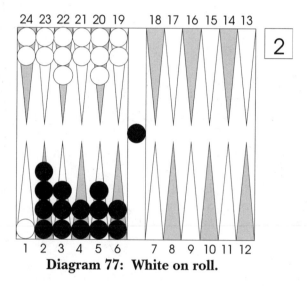

Diagram 77: White on roll.

61. White doubles to 4.
For the first time in the game, White is a favorite, and Snellings immediately doubles! Is the double correct? Can Black accept? Let's take a closer look.

Grouping Numbers Together
To understand the situation, we have to take a close look at how White's different numbers play next turn. Grouping similar numbers together, White's 36 possible throws fall into three main categories:

• Group A - White's best numbers. With 11 of his 36 rolls, White rolls a 6 and hops Black's prime. These numbers are terrific for White. He becomes more than a 95% favorite in the game. In this group, White's very happy if he has already doubled.

• Group B - White's worst numbers. With 14 of his 36 numbers, White breaks a point in his board, giving Black a chance to enter. These numbers are all fives except 65, the 43 roll, and medium doubles, 44, 33, and 22. After any of these rolls, the game becomes a race to see who can first roll a 6. With Black now the first to shoot, he becomes the favorite in the game.

• Group C - In-between numbers. With the 11 remaining numbers, small numbers like 41, 31, and 21, White's position deteriorates but his board remains closed. After a roll like 32, for instance, White's board will break on the next turn on any roll that does not contain a 6.

So, can Black take? The answer is yes. In fact, the take is quite easy. Black becomes a favorite in the game as soon as White's board breaks, and it's more likely that will happen next turn than that White will escape.

Can White double? Actually White should wait a turn. The inducement to double is that White can become a huge favorite if he rolls a 6. If not, he becomes a slight underdog. On balance, White does a little better waiting. The doubling cube can be very useful to White in variations like the following:

• White breaks his 19-point.
• Black stays out.
• White rolls a 6, leaping into the outfield.
• Black rolls a 6, coming in on the 19-point and waiting for White to come around.

In these variations, White will be very happy that he can offer a powerful double later at an optimal time.

This particular sort of position arises fairly frequently. A good rule of thumb is this:

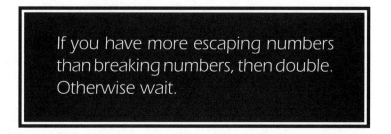

If you have more escaping numbers than breaking numbers, then double. Otherwise wait.

62. Black takes.

63. White 61: 1/8
A fine roll. Now the game is just about over.

64. Black can't move.

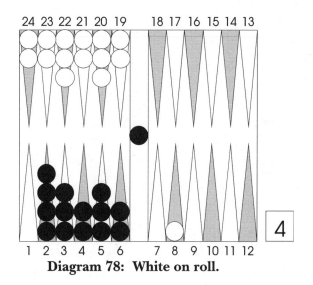

Diagram 78: White on roll.

65. White 41: 8/13
Notice that White leaves his spares on the 20 and 22-points where they are. For the safest possible bearoff, you want your spares on the high points in your board rather than the low points. This will give you maximum flexibility for playing your later rolls.

66. Black can't move.

67. White 54: 13/22
A forced play. White hasn't achieved a particularly good bearoff because he has an odd number (five) checkers on his two highest points. This will force him to expose a blot if his next roll is 55 or 66. However, given his rolls, there was no way to avoid this situation.

68. Black can't move.

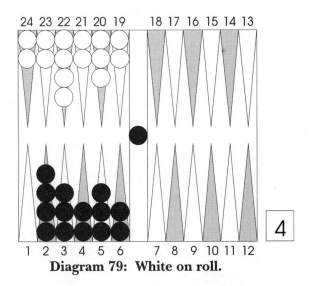

Diagram 79: White on roll.

69. White 11: 22/off 20/21
Small doubles are very useful in the bearoff since they allow you to rearrange your spares as you please. Now White has an even number of men on his high points.

70. Black can't move.

71. White 31: 21/off

72. Black can't move.

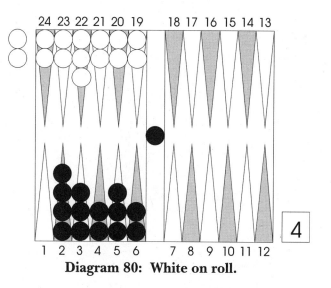

Diagram 80: White on roll.

73. White 21: 19/20 19/21
This play is an error.

Safety Versus Gammon Chances

Although it's slightly safer than the simple 22/off (because it allows Black to enter immediately and get out of White's hair), safety is not the only consideration. It's wrong because of two other factors:

- It's not the best play for the gammon. White has some small chances of winning a gammon in this position, and playing 22/off maximizes those chances by keeping a closed board.

- It's not the best play for the race. Opening the 19-point

gives Black the chance of rolling 66 and getting back in the race. 22/off bears off another checker and makes the race even more secure.

The net result is that 22/off is slightly better, although the plays are close.

74. Black stays out.

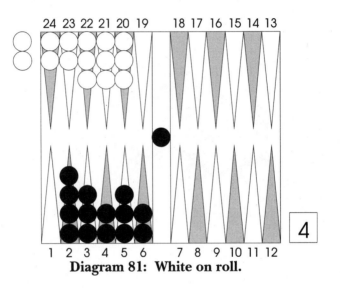

Diagram 81: White on roll.

75. White 21: 20/21 22/24
Again, White makes a slight error. This play is safer than the alternative 22/off. However, 22/off is slightly better because it leaves a position which is nonetheless quite safe and which is much more likely to win a gammon.

Incidentally, the safest play of all is the simple 20/22 21/22, which, however, is least likely to win a gammon.

In most bearoffs where the possibility of contact still remains, safety is only one goal. This has to be balanced against the value of more dangerous plays which have a better chance of winning a gammon. These decisions are often quite difficult, because the chances of either losing or winning a gammon are pretty small.

When in doubt, bear off aggressively.

76. Black 66: Bar/1
A great shot, but Black will need a couple of more to get back in the game.

77. White 51: 20/off 24/off

78. Black 55: 5/off(3) 6/1
Another great shot! White has 11 checkers left against Black's 12, so he's still a big favorite. But Black is now within striking distance.

79. White 32: 22/off 23/off

80. Black 31: 3/off 1/off

81. White 61: 20/off 24/off

82. Black 62: 6/off 2/off

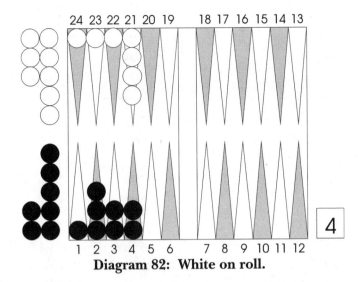

Diagram 82: White on roll.

83. White 41: 21/off 24/off

> In general, you should always bear checkers off with direct numbers rather than try to improve your distribution for future rolls.

The extra checkers off are permanent, while the improved distribution may never matter. White's actual play is considerable better than 21/off 21/22, which some players might have chosen.

84. Black 65: 4/off(2)

85. White 52: 21/off 23/off
A single double now could win the game for Black.

86. Black 52: 3/off 2/off

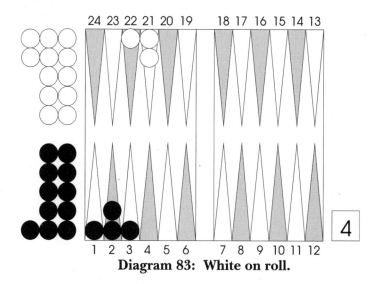

Diagram 83: White on roll.

87. White 51: 21/off 22/23
In the bearoff, try to keep checkers spread out on different points. White's play lets him bear off both checkers next turn with 23 (out of 36) numbers. The blunder 21/off 21/22, putting both men on the 22-point, only lets White get off with 17 throws.

88. Black 51: 3/off 1/off

89. White 42: 21/off 23/off
Perfect! This roll might have lost the game had White misplayed roll 87.

White wins 4 points.

Summary:
Sylvester gets off to an early edge, doubles at just the right time, and then displays perfect technique in pinning Snellings into an ace-point game. Study Sylvester's plays in this phase of the game carefully, since this situation arises frequently in backgammon.

Snellings finally works up some counterplay with a timely throw of double-aces. Realizing that he needs to build a prime quickly to get more than a simple ace-point game, he creates counterchances with excellent plays at moves 29 and 31. Snelling's prime holds and he is eventually able to free his back men.

Look at the last few moves of the game for some lessons in balancing speed and safety when bearing off against contact. These plays are difficult and will repay dividends later with careful study.

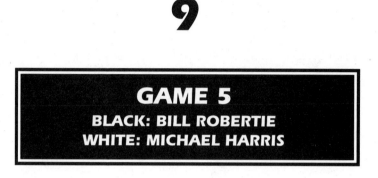

9

GAME 5
BLACK: BILL ROBERTIE
WHITE: MICHAEL HARRIS

Michael Harris was one of the top English players during the 1980s.

This game was played in the round of 16 at the World Championship in Monte Carlo in 1987. The match was to 21 points, and Robertie held a 9-8 lead.

1. White 64: 1/11
One of the two popular ways of opening the game with a 64. This move mostly escapes one checker and puts some pressure on White's outfield, making it difficult for Black to escape a checker.

The other play, which I prefer, is to split to the bar-point with 1/7, then bring a builder into play with 12/16. My idea in the opening is to fight for key anchoring/blocking points, while postponing running until later.

2. Black 42: 24/20 13/11*
Hitting is clear, of course. With the four, I like to split to the 20-point while my opponent is on the bar, since he can't then make a point on my head unless he rolls doubles. Meanwhile, I've started a valuable anchor and controlled the outfield as well. I'm off to a good start in this game.

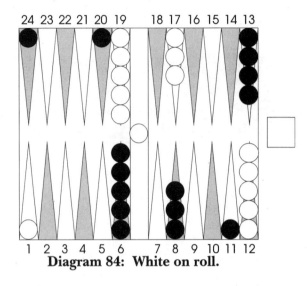

Diagram 84: White on roll.

3. White 61: Bar/7
A poor shot, but there's no other way to play it. White can't play 12/18 since the checker would be exposed to a double shot. By moving out to the 7-point, he prevents me from hitting and making an inner point at the same time.

> In general, a loose six in the opening should be played to the opposing bar-point rather than to your own bar-point. The downside is less, while the upside is greater.

4. Black 62: 13/7* 13/11
I hit with the six, while the two makes a new point.

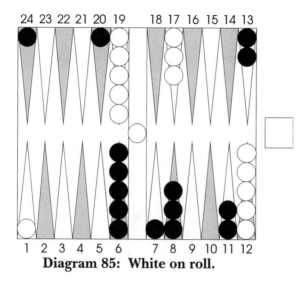

Diagram 85: White on roll.

5. White 53: Bar/5 17/20*

White enters and hits, fighting for control of both 5-points. In modern backgammon, the 5-point is the key to successful opening strategy. You must battle for the 5-points rather than surrendering one or another to your opponent. This is true even if you risk falling behind in the race as a result.

A passive play like Bar/22 13/8 leaves White worse off on both sides of the board while still facing annihilation if Black can get an attack going. In the long run, actively fighting for the 5-points is the least risky way to play the opening.

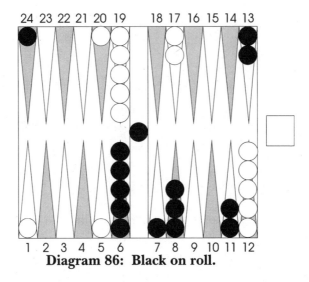

Diagram 86: Black on roll.

6. Black 42: Bar/23 24/20*

Here Black has a choice of **which** 5-point to fight for.

Which 5 - Point?

Besides the play I made, fighting for White's 5-point, I could have played Bar/21 7/5*, fighting for my 5-point. In this case, the play I made is better since it guarantees a gain in the race while contesting a point.

Remember this basic rule:

> A play that does two good things is better than a play that just does one good thing.

7. White 51: Bar/5 19/20*

White makes one 5-point while fighting for the other and unstacking his pile on the 19-point. A nice roll.

8. Black 64: Bar/21 13/7

Not the best, as I really wanted to hit back on the 20-point. Now White may be able to grab both 5-points, a great result for him. As a consolation prize, I get my bar point. I didn't like giving up the midpoint, but the 7-point is key to building a blockade against White's back men.

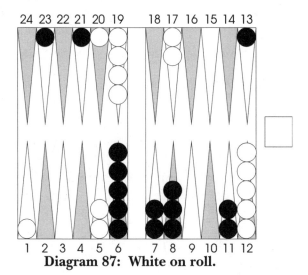

24 23 22 21 20 19　18 17 16 15 14 13

1　2　3　4　5　6　　7　8　9　10 11 12

Diagram 87:　White on roll.

9. White 21: 19/21* 20/21

White has a bunch of choices with this move. His play is obvious, making the 21-point while leaving no shots. Besides this move, White could try:

• 12/13* 19/21*, hitting two men. This play will look great if Black doesn't roll a four or a five coming back. Otherwise, it won't accomplish much. This is probably the weakest reasonable choice.

• 19/20 19/21*, making the 20-point. This play has the great virtue of making the most valuable point on the board, at the cost of leaving a return shot. The real merit of the play is that this is likely to be a very long game

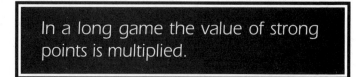

In a long game the value of strong points is multiplied.

- A strong point, by definition, nullifies certain possibilities for your opponent each roll. The longer the game, the more effective the strong points are.

To Hit Or Not To Hit

- Another possibility is 19/20 12/14, hitting no one, but diversifying off the midpoint. This is actually my first choice. The hit here doesn't accomplish much since Black has no threats which need to be prevented. The non-hitting play actually gives White the best board control of any play.

The non-hit is a hard play to find, since there are so many hitting plays available.

When you've already achieved a good position, a structural play may be more important than a loose hit.

10. Black stays out.

11. White 52: 12/17 12/14
White brings more builders to bear on the 20-point and the 18-point. He also completes the job of unstacking the midpoint and bringing his checkers into play.

Right now, the game is about even. White has the better structure, but Black leads in the race and has the makings of a blockade.

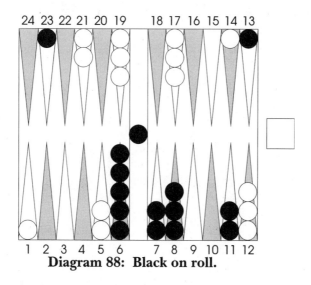

Diagram 88: Black on roll.

12. Black 55: Bar/15 23/13
A nice shot, and my position improves dramatically. I remake the midpoint and escape the last checker. A lot now hinges on whether White can now hit with a one or a three. If White hits, we will still have a complex game. If White misses, the game will become a holding position with White anchored on the 5-point and waiting to get a shot later in the game.

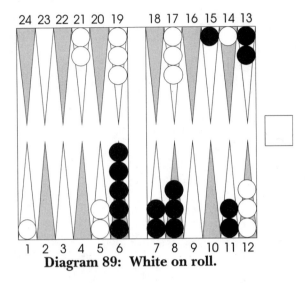

Diagram 89: White on roll.

13. White 63: 12/15* 14/20

White hits with the three and then has a choice on how to play the six. He can't move his back men, and breaking the midpoint with 12/18 doesn't look appetizing. The choice is between the safe 15/21 and the bold 14/20.

Bold Play Versus Safe Play

Some 20 years ago, Paul Magriel, in his great work *Backgammon*, developed the criteria for deciding between a safe play and a bold play. Those criteria were a breakthrough at the time and have since been adopted by all the top players. They remain as valid today as when he wrote his masterwork.

Briefly, here are Magriel's criteria:

> **(1)** Compare the strength of the inner boards. If your inner board is stronger, make a bold play. If his inner board is stronger, make a safe play.

Here White has the stronger inner board. This argues for a bold play.

(2) See who is ahead in the race. If you are behind in the race, make a bold play. Otherwise, make a safe play.

Here the pip count is White 155, Black 141 after White's play. White trails in the race, so a bold play is called for.

(3) Who has more men back? If you have more men back, you are inclined to play boldly. If your opponent has more men back, you are inclined to play safe.

Here White has three men back, Black only one man back (on the bar). This argues for a bold play from White.

All three criteria argue for White to play boldly. The overall strategic idea is that White, behind in the race with more men back, is very likely to have to play some sort of holding game or back game in order to win unless he can quickly build a countering prime against Black's single checker.

Since he must build this prime quickly, however, he wants to slot the key points rather than wait to roll them naturally, which rates to take several moves longer. Hence the slot is best. Very nice play by Harris.

14. Black 41: Bar/20*
Oh well. Unlike chess, in backgammon you only get rewarded for your good plays a percentage of the time. White made a good play, but it didn't work. That's backgammon.

15. White stays out.
White danced. Should Black double?

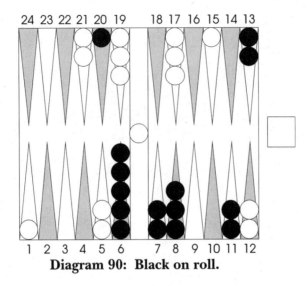

24 23 22 21 20 19   18 17 16 15 14 13

1 2 3 4 5 6   7 8 9 10 11 12

Diagram 90: Black on roll.

The answer is no. Black has an advantage, since he's way ahead in the race. But the game could still get very complicated, and Black has no home-board points yet. A double would be very premature.

16. Black 31: 8/7 6/3
This roll shows just how quickly a good-looking position can deteriorate if you have no inner board points.

I can't move the back checker, so I have to leave a blot some-where. The right idea is to preserve all the points I own and throw away one of the useless checkers stacked on the 6-point. When that gets hit, it may reenter the game and go to a more constructive position.

17. White 42: Bar/4 1/3*
Clear-cut. White catches up a little in the race.

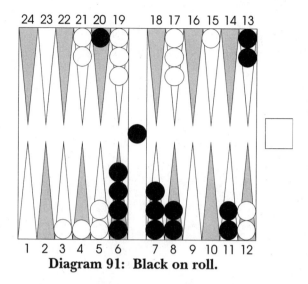

Diagram 91: Black on roll.

18. Black 65: Bar/20 13/7

The five is forced, then I need to find a good six. Since there are no "good" sixes, I need to find the least damaging six. Playing 20/14 is out of the question: I need the anchor here, and White would have ones, threes, fives, and twos to hit me if I ran.

Playing 7/1 puts a checker out of play, which I really don't want to do in this complex position. It seems like I'm going to need all 15 of my checkers in play to win the game.

That leaves 13/7 as the least evil choice. I don't like giving up the midpoint, but at least my 11-point serves some of the functions of a midpoint.

19. White 41: 12/13*/17

White hits and makes a little more progress. He doesn't really like putting the checker on the 17-point, but 12/13* 12/16 looks a little too loose with nebulous benefits.

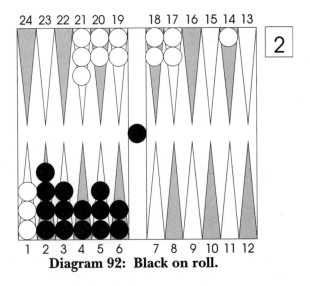

Diagram 92: Black on roll.

20. Black 51: Bar/24 20/15*

An interesting roll. If I play Bar/20, my only ace is 7/6. That's certainly unconstructive. On the other hand, since I'm still ahead in the race, I'm looking for a chance to make a break for home, and this could be my best shot.

Breaking the anchor now is much less dangerous than it was last turn. Because of the duplication, White only has ones and threes to hit me.

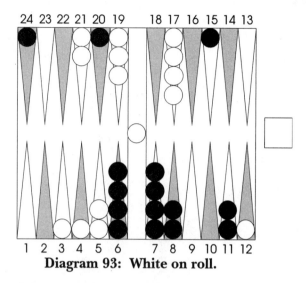

Diagram 93: White on roll.

21. White 42: Bar/4 3/5

White can't hit, so he builds the 4-point, giving him a 4-5 back game, and moves his spare to the 5-point, ready to leap out with fours and fives.

Recirculation

When playing a back game, it's vital *not* to get extra checkers stuck in your opponent's inner board. Checkers not needed to hold vital points should keep flowing into the outer boards. This process is called recirculation, and it's vital to maintaining good timing.

22. Black 61: 20/14 15/14

Black makes the 14-point and takes aim at his 9-point and 10-point. White wants to recirculate; Black wants to shut the door on recirculation. If Black can make the 9 or 10-points, recirculation gets more difficult and White's game could get cramped.

23. White 51: 5/10 17/18

With two back-game points made and recirculation easy for the time being, White has no worries about being hit. This is a game

White is going to have to win later. Meanwhile, White can just slot the points he wants and see if he can make them. Good back game play by Harris.

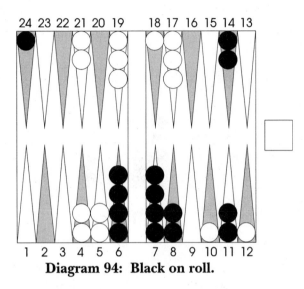

Diagram 94: Black on roll.

24. Black 65: 24/18* 7/2
The hit with the six is clear. Although White doesn't really mind being hit, I can't allow myself to get blocked in. If that happens, I could still lose going forward.

The play of the five should be less clear. Why deliberately sacrifice a checker with 7/2, when I could just keep my back checker moving with 18/13? To understand this play, we'll have to look a little more deeply into back game strategy.

Back Game Strategy
First, let's look at what happens if I try to rush my men home as quickly as possible, let's say after 24/18*/13. White will reenter, perhaps on my 1 or 2-point, and leave his blots on the 10 and 12-points. He'll try to slot the 20-point or the 22-point, building his board quickly. In order to get my checkers on the 14 and 13-points home, I'll need to hit one of his blots, perhaps both blots.

These checkers will enter my board easily, perhaps making a third anchor on the 2-point or the 3-point. After that, where will I put my checkers? I'll have to make big stacks on the 6, 7, and 8-points, while perhaps dumping a blot or two on whatever points are left open in my board. Meanwhile, White will build the 20 and 22-points.

This scenario doesn't look too promising for me. If I'm lucky, I might roll some small doubles and clear some of my points successfully. If I'm real lucky, I'll even win a gammon this way. But more likely, I'll get a checker hit and stuck behind White's prime at a time when my own position is in ruins. That's the basic strategy for a successful back game, and here, with no home board at all, I'm vulnerable to that strategy.

I need a better plan of attack. Fortunately for me, there's one available.

Take a look at my spare checkers on the 6-point and 7-point. Right now, those spares are useless to me. I can't use them to make the 4-point or the 5-point since White won't break those points until he can hit a winning shot. Making the 1-point or the 2-point will put them out of play.

Suppose I could move those checkers backwards. If I could move them back to the 13-point or 15-point, they would become builders for the key 9-point and 10-point. If I could close those points, I'd have White squeezed! Then there might be a real chance of trapping some White checkers behind my prime and keeping them trapped until his board collapsed.

How do I move checkers backward? By recirculating them, just as White has been doing with his checkers. So I'm going to start dumping those spares onto the open points in my board. If White hits them when he reenters from the bar, I'll come around the board and take aim at the really important points in the position – the 9-point and the 10-point.

158

This strategy has some built-in risks. I might get some checkers caught in White's home board just as he makes a small block. If I roll awkwardly at that point, I might lose a prime versus prime game.

But that's a risk I'm willing to take. I'm going to create an extraordinarily complex position, and I'm expecting to outplay my opponent when that happens. As for the possibility of bad luck, I'll take my chances. That's part of the game of backgammon.

25. White 63: Bar/3 12/18*
White enters, missing the blot on the deuce, and naturally rehits.

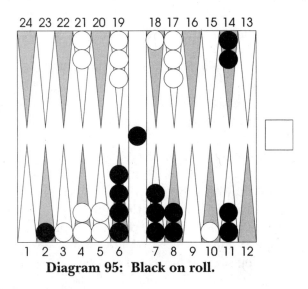

Diagram 95: Black on roll.

26. Black 61: Bar/18*
A good roll, preventing White from blocking me and sending another White checker back. To make my strategy work, I want to hit White, despite the fact that White's playing a back game. It's the only way I can get my checkers recirculated. That's what makes this position different from a normal back game.

In a normal back game, White is trying to be hit and I am trying to avoid hitting. In this position, White is better off not hitting or being hit. However, many players in White's position would not realize this.

27. White 51: Bar/5 17/18*
A mistake, for the reasons outlined in the last comment. I think White should have played Bar/5 19/20, just building his board.

28. Black 63: Bar/16

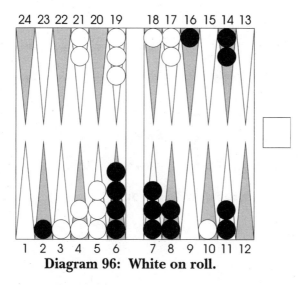

24 23 22 21 20 19   18 17 16 15 14 13

1 2 3 4 5 6   7 8 9 10 11 12
Diagram 96: White on roll.

29. White 51: 10/16*
This is a serious error. White doesn't suspect what's happening and is playing into Black's hands. Instead he should play 5/10 3/4. Making the 10-point would provide a bridge for White's spares to circulate into the outfield, while playing 3/4 would get the spare ready to leap with a five or a six.

30. Black 43: Bar/18*
As we've seen before, I'm happy to keep hitting. It will provide me with more opportunities to recirculate checkers.

31. White 31: Bar/3 17/18*

As before, I think White is pursuing the wrong idea. He can't contain the Black checker, and he has enough men back to ensure good timing. Instead he should play Bar/3 19/20.

32. Black stays out.

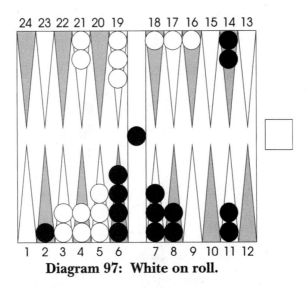

Diagram 97: White on roll.

33. White 65: 4/10 5/10

A great shot, which White plays correctly. By grabbing a point in the middle of Black's prime, he gives his back checkers a permanent avenue of escape. This is much better than making the 22-point, his other option.

34. Black 54: Bar/16*

I'm continuing with my plan, although White's last roll was a real setback for me. Still, the more White men I send back, the better.

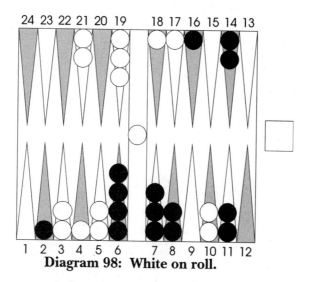

Diagram 98: White on roll.

35. White 33: Bar/3 10/16* 17/20

A big mistake. The loose hit breaks the key connecting point that White made last turn. If White can't quickly remake the 10-point, he could be in serious trouble.

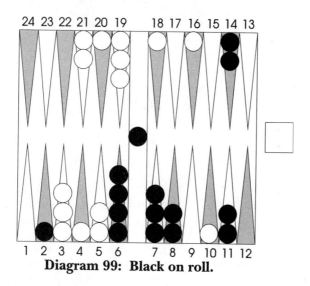

Diagram 99: Black on roll.

36. Black 52: Bar/20* 6/4*

Hitting on the 20-point is clear. I could continue on and hit on the 18-point, but my actual play is better. By hitting with one of the dead spares on the 6-point, I have a chance to reactivate that checker. Since White now has two men on the bar, he can't avoid hitting me if he rolls a two or a four.

37. White 64: Bar/4*

Forced, but now I have another checker in play.

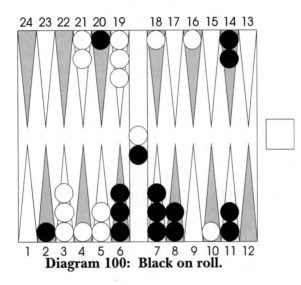

Diagram 100: Black on roll.

38. Black 11: Bar/24 14/13 11/10*(2)

A great shot which accomplishes a bunch of good things:

• Hitting another checker will force White to hit me if he rolls a deuce.

• Switching from the 11-point to the 10-point brings my points closer together, giving me a stronger blockade.

• Splitting from the 14-point to the 13-point gives me two builders for the key 9-point, the next blocking point I want to make.

39. White 52: Bar/5 Bar/2*

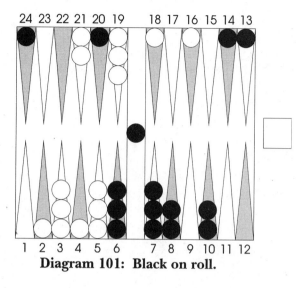

Diagram 101: Black on roll.

40. Black doubles to 2.

I thought this was a very strong double and just barely, if at all, a take. My plan has been very successful. I've sent eight checkers back and broken the connection between the two halves of White's position. I've managed to recirculate two of the four dead checkers I used to have on the 6-point and 7-point; I might still be able to recirculate the other two. And if I make the 9-point, my game will be completely crushing.

The argument against doubling is that many players overestimate the strength of back games and tend to take too often. Following that logic, I might be able to take a roll, improve my position some more, and still get a take later on. But it's risky trying to get too greedy. I've got good chances for a gammon this game, so I'm going to get the cube moving now.

41. White takes.

Courageous but very dangerous. Still, White does have some play left. I might have taken also, but very reluctantly.

42. Black 32: Bar/22 6/4*

Playing 20/18* with the deuce is a little safer for me, but I want to recirculate yet another checker.

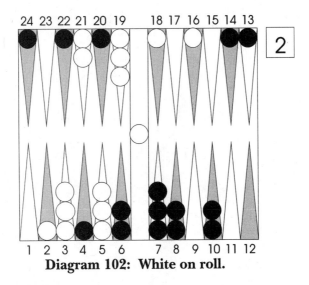

Diagram 102: White on roll.

43. White 61: Bar/1 3/9

Another small mistake. White sticks a checker on the very point I want to make. This would be all right if White were buttoned up around the board, but unfortunately he has four other blots besides this one. If I can hit on the 9-point, I'll probably hit somewhere else as well; with two White checkers on the bar, White won't be able to hit me back on the 9-point.

A better idea was Bar/1 5/11, or even Bar/1 16/22*.

44. Black 42: 13/9* 20/18*

As predicted. In many variations I'll be able to cover the 9-point next turn, with a crushing block.

45. White 43: Bar/3 Bar/4*

A good shot, putting me on the bar. That cuts down on my cover numbers.

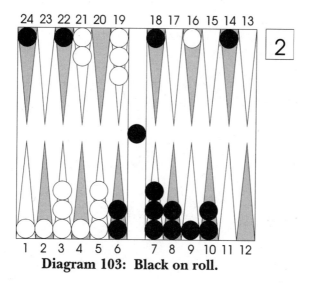

Diagram 103: Black on roll.

46. Black 21: Bar/23 10/9
I can't make five in a row with this number, but at least I can make four consecutive points.

47. White 62: 4/10* 16/18*
A fine shot. Now White has some time to get a few men beyond the barricades.

48. Black 22: Bar/23(2) 14/10*
A great comeback shot. I don't want White making the 10-point, so I hit there, rather than on the 18-point.

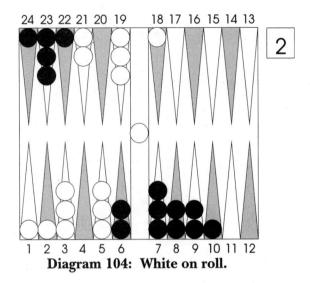

24 23 22 21 20 19   18 17 16 15 14 13

2

1 2 3 4 5 6   7 8 9 10 11 12
Diagram 104: White on roll.

49. White 11: Bar/2 3/4(2)
I don't like this move, although it looks consistent with the previous play. White's just been given an unlikely opportunity, and he needs to take advantage of it.

Better is Bar/1 18/20 19/20! By making a 3-point block of his own, White would give Black a few problems. Suddenly Black's small numbers don't play well with five of his checkers in White's home board. Black needs to keep his back checkers moving, and even a 3-point block could prove a real nuisance.

50. Black 42: 22/18*/16
Black hits and moves to the 16-point to connect to the slot on the 10-point. If I'm not hit, I can make a 5-point prime with any six. That should lock up the game.

51. White 21: Bar/3

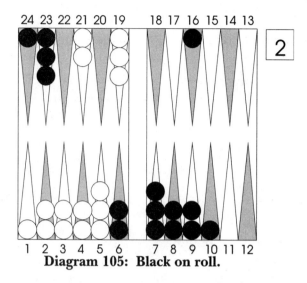

Diagram 105: Black on roll.

52. Black 64: 16/10 24/20
Making five in a row gives me an iron grip on the position. My next job is to destroy White's forward position.

One thing I don't want to do at this point is hit any more checkers. Up to now, I've been hitting checkers with the idea of keeping White off balance and uncoordinated, unable to prevent me from making the key outside points. That job is done; I've divided White's position into two halves, with five checkers in his home board and 10 behind my prime.

If White could get all 15 of his checkers sent into my inner board, he'd have a pretty good game again. As I bore in and took down my points, he'd release his checkers into the outfield and build a prime somewhere in the outer boards. Then he'd be a real threat if he hit a checker.

Mopping Up
Ideally, I want to keep his army separated into two halves, so that the pieces can't cooperate. My next goals are:

- Release my back checkers.

- Make the 11-point, for a full 6-point prime.

- Don't hit any more checkers; hope that White rolls some fours and fives so that his checkers on the 19-point move down to the 23-point and 24-point.

53. White 42: 1/5 2/4
White must get checkers to the 5-point, so he can release as many as possible with sixes.

54. Black 32: 23/18
Heading toward the 11-point.

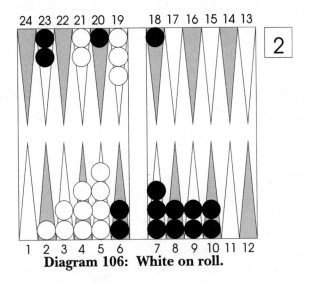

Diagram 106: White on roll.

55. White 62: 5/11 2/4
I would play 5/11 3/5. Releasing as many checkers as soon as possible is the key. Trying to keep three back game points is probably too optimistic.

56. Black 43: 18/11*
A good shot. Fighting for the 11-point is top priority.

57. White 52: Bar/5 19/21
White is trying to hold onto the 3-point as long as possible.

58. Black 53: 23/18 20/17
This gives me sixes and sevens to make the 11-point.

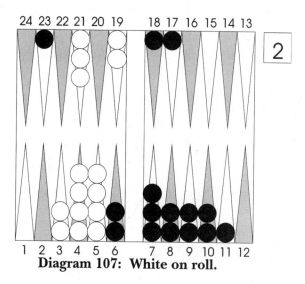

Diagram 107: White on roll.

59. White 32: 19/22 21/23*
We call this the *kamikaze play*. White breaks apart his home board in an attempt to get all his checkers back. It won't work if Black knows what he's doing, which isn't always the case.

60. Black 21: Bar/24 18/16
Avoiding the hit, and getting ready to cover the 11 with sixes and fives.

61. White 55: 19/24*
Forced, but not all that bad. Notice that White can't play any more fives or fours, which slows down his collapse.

62. Black 41: Bar/24*/20
I didn't want to hit, but I can't avoid it.

63. White 21: Bar/2 21/22

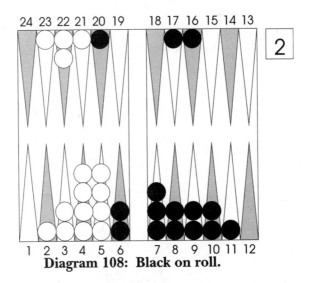

Diagram 108: Black on roll.

64. Black 41: 16/11
Click! The last door shuts. Now it's just a question of how far White will have to advance before I open up my prime. Large numbers are now good for White, since he can't play them.

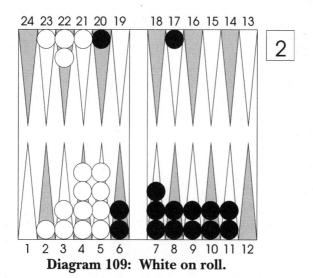

Diagram 109: White on roll.

65. White 31: 21/24 2/3
Playing this way kills threes. Now White only has to play ones and twos; with luck, he can preserve his remaining points until my prime gives way.

66. Black 42: 17/13 20/18
Small numbers are good for me as I can hold my prime longer.

67. White 11: 3/5 4/5 22/23
That uses up a lot of White's spare pips. He can only tolerate one more deuce.

68. Black 42: 13/9 18/16
Another good throw.

69. White 62: 3/5
Not the right deuce, I think. I would have played 22/24, keeping the extra back point.

70. Black 22: 16/8

71. White 64: can't move.

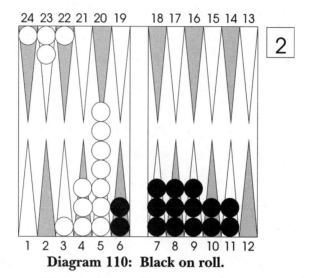

Diagram 110: Black on roll.

72. Black 43: 9/6 7/3*
I'm just trying to keep my prime as long as possible. I don't care whether the checker on the 3-point gets hit or not.

73. White 61: Bar/1

74. Black 22: 11/9 11/7 3/1*
My prime finally cracks, but it's done most of its work. Hitting on the 1-point makes 66 a bad, rather than a great number for White.

75. White 52: Bar/5 22/24
Forced.

76. Black 31: 7/3

77. White 54: can't move.

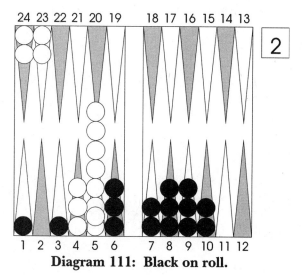

Diagram 111: Black on roll.

78. Black 32: 9/7 6/3
Keeping the 5-prime for as long as possible is still useful. If White rolls an ace before he rolls a six, he'll have to make yet another concession.

79. White 33: can't move.

80. Black 65: 8/2 7/2

81. White 51: 4/5
White rolls his ace and has to strip the 4-point. That gives me another avenue to attack his position.

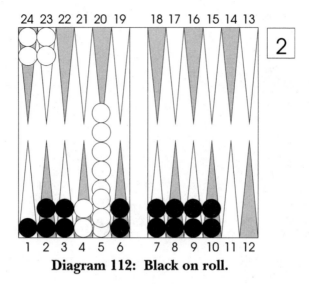

Diagram 112: Black on roll.

82. Black 64: 7/3 7/1
This is it.

Attacking A Stripped Point

By breaking my prime in the middle, I force White to play any three from the 4-point. Any three except 63 will break that point down.

83. White 31: 4/7 4/5
Oops. Now White's down to a single holding point, which I should get by easily. In addition, I now have great gammon chances.

84. Black 66: 10/4(2) 9/3(2)
Good for clearing points and good for winning the gammon.

85. White 51: 7/13
Gets that checker out of danger, but White is still hurting. He'll need to hit a shot just to have a chance at saving the gammon.

86. Black 43: 6/2 6/3
I can't clear the 8-point, so the 6-point will have to do.

87. White 62: 5/11 13/15

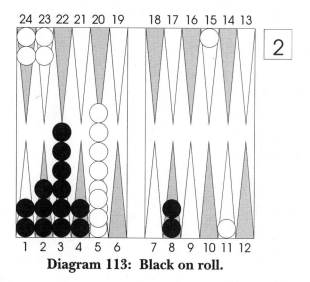

Diagram 113: Black on roll.

88. Black 54: 8/4 8/3
That's it. I now need 15 crossovers to bear off all my checkers, while White needs 31 to get off the gammon. It's a lock.

Black won a gammon and 4 points.

Summary:
This game began with a struggle for both 5-points. White won the battle for the defensive 5-point, but had to concede ground in the race. However, Black was not able to build any inner-board points. During the hitting battle which followed, White was able to construct a 4-5 holding position.

Rather than play a back game where White had excellent timing, Black recirculated some checkers to build up greater outfield control. White was willing to give up key outside connecting points to attempt to build a prime of his own. Eventually, Black was able to consolidate control of the outfield and build a prime, trapping 10 of White's men. When his remaining men were forced onto the low points in his board, White lost any serious winning chances.

10

NEXT STEPS

Improving Your Game

After you've finished reading this book, you'd probably like to try your hand at playing in a backgammon tournament. That's not hard to do. There are local clubs all around the country, running tournaments on a weekly or a monthly basis. Visit a club near you and introduce yourself to the director. Most clubs run tournaments in separate sections, one for beginners and one for more experienced players, so don't worry if you've never played in a tournament before. Just hop in and give it a try!

For a list of clubs and tournaments around the country, send $1.00 to The Gammon Press, P.O. Box 294, Arlington, MA 02174. Most major cities have one or more active clubs.

Backgammon On The Internet

In the unlikely event that you live far away from a local club, or if you just prefer the idea of electronic play to face-to-face competition, it's now possible to play backgammon matches over the Internet. In fact, there are now two separate Internet backgammon clubs in operation!

For the best graphics and quickest response time, try GamesGrid. Use your web browser to log on to http://zola.cyberarts.com, and follow the instructions for downloading the GamesGrid software. Then just follow the directions to connect.

Another choice is FIBS, the First Internet Backgammon Server. Use telnet to reach the address "fibs.com 4321". You'll get a screen with a set of instructions that tell you how to log on.

Improving Your Game

I'm often asked, "Is there any magic to getting good at backgammon?" My answer is yes. There are two magic ingredients: Study and Practice. If you've read this book, you've already made a good start on studying. You'll still want to review the five games several times. Each time you play the game over, you'll pick up some new ideas.

But studying is only half the battle. You still have to practice. Without steady practice, without testing yourself and your growing abilities, you won't really absorb the lessons of this book. So find a local club, visit steadily, and play as much as you can. You'll be amazed at your steady progress. Good luck!

11

IMPROVING YOUR GAME

I'm often asked, "Is there any magic to getting good at backgammon?" My answer is yes. There are two magic ingredients: Study and Practice. If you've read this book, you've already made a good start on studying. You'll still want to review the five games several times. Each time you play the game over, you'll pick up some new ideas.

But studying is only half the battle. You still have to practice. Without steady practice, without testing yourself and your growing abilities, you won't really absorb the lessons of this book. So find a local club, visit steadily, and play as much as you can. You'll be amazed at your steady progress. Good luck!

GLOSSARY

Backgammon is full of its own colorful terminology. Here are some terms you will want to remember:

Advanced Anchor - An anchor on the opponent's 4-point or 5-point.

Anchor - A defensive point in the opponent's inner board.

Back Game - A defensive position in which the defending side holds two or more points in the opponent's **inner board**. The best back game points to hold are the 1 and 3, the 2 and 3, and the 2 and 4. The worst back games are the 1 and 4 or the 1 and 5. Any position with three back game points is very strong.

Back Position - The defensive position on your opponent's side of the board. In our diagrams, Black's back position would be his points in White's home board, points 19-24.

Barabino - A roll of 54 from the bar, used to make the defensive 20-point.

Bar - The vertical strip running down the center of the board between the 6 and 7-points on one side and the 18 and 19-points on the other. Checkers which have been hit have to go to the bar. They must reenter the game next turn in the opponent's home board.

Bar Point - In our diagrams, Black's bar-point is the 7-point. White's bar-point is the 18-point.

Bearoff - The section of the game where players bear off checkers from their inner boards in the final race to victory.

Builder - A checker placed so that it bears on vital points which need to be made in the future.

Connectivity - The arrangement of checkers so that they are in direct range (six pips or less) of each other. Connected checkers defend each other and are easily made into points.

Crawford Game - In tournament play, the Crawford Game occurs when one side is one point from victory. In this situation, the doubling cube cannot be used. After the Crawford Game, if the match is still in progress, the cube can be used normally.

Crossover - The movement of a checker from one quadrant of the board to another, or off the board from the home board.

Crossover Count - The total number of crossovers required to bear off all checkers. Once all the checkers are in the home board, the crossover count is 15 or less.

Dead Cube - In a tournament match, a cube is said to be dead when the player owning the cube has no reason to ever double. For example, a player who is two points from winning the match and who owns a 2-cube will never double, since he can win the match with the cube at its current level.

Direct Shot - A shot at a checker six or fewer pips away, so that the checker can be hit with a single number on the dice.

Disengage - To break all contact, so that the position becomes a pure race.

Diversification - Playing your move so that on the following turn you will have different numbers on the dice to accomplish different objectives. A good offensive maneuver. See also **duplication**.

Double - To turn the doubling cube one notch, thereby doubling the value of the game. The player who has been doubled has the option of accepting the cube and playing for twice the value, or declining and paying his opponent the original stake. Once a player has accepted a double, he "owns" the cube and only he can double again.

Downside - What you lose if you take a risk and it backfires. See also **upside**.

Duplication - Playing your move so that your opponent needs the same numbers on the dice to accomplish different objectives, thus ensuring that he has fewer rolls working for him. A good defensive maneuver. See also **diversification**.

Front Position - The collection of blocking/attacking points in your own home board. In our diagrams, Black's front position is his points in the area of points 1-8.

Full Prime - Six points in a row.

Gammon - Winning the game by bearing off all your checkers before your opponent has borne off any checkers. The player winning a gammon wins twice the value of the cube.

Going Forward - To attack by building forward points, constructing a prime, and putting your opponent on the bar.

Home Board - The quadrant of the board to which a player needs to move his checkers for the bearoff. In our diagrams, points 1-6 are Black's home board, points 19-24 are White's home board. Also known as the **Inner Board**.

Inner Board - see **Home Board**.

Kamikaze Play - Breaking points in one's own inner board in hopes of getting the checkers recirculated. A back game strategy.

Key Point - A vital point which conveys a big advantage to whichever player can make it first.

Killing Numbers - To play your roll in such a way that some numbers on the dice can't be played next turn. A useful way to slow down the deterioration of your position in a priming battle.

Long Shot - An unlikely but powerful roll. The chance of rolling a single double, like 66, is 35-1 against. The chance of rolling a single non-double, like 65, is 17-1 against.

Losing Your Market - To have both a very solid advantage and some threats which, if executed, will force your opponent to drop a later double.

Midpoint - Black's midpoint is the 13-point in our diagrams. White's midpoint is the 12-point. A good strategic point to hold in the early game since it provides a landing spot for the back checkers and controls the outer board.

Money Game - A game played for money, in which the cube can always be turned, if available. Tournament play differs from money play in that many situations arise where a player can't (or shouldn't) turn the cube. Good tournament players must be alert to these situations.

Nullo Play - A play that can't be better than an alternative play, no matter what the sequence of dice rolls is. Making a nullo play is the worst possible logical blunder.

Outer Board - The points numbered 7-18, which are not part of either side's inner board.

Permanent Asset - An asset which can't go away after a single lucky throw by the opponent.

Pip Count - The total number of pips needed to be rolled on the dice to bear off all your checkers. It's calculated by multiplying the number of a point by the number of checkers on that point, and adding the totals together. At the start of the game, both sides' pip count is 167.

Prime - A collection of consecutive points blocking in your opponent's men. Six points in a row is called a **full prime**, and is the strongest possible blockade since the opponent can't jump over it with any possible number.

Recirculation - Keeping checkers in play by having them hit and then reentering the game from the opponent's home board.

Slot - Placing a blot on a point with the idea of making the point next turn.

Structural Play - A move which builds strong points.

Timing - The ability to hold your key points while you are waiting to get a shot. In general, the farther behind in the race you are, the better your timing.

Undoubled Gammon - In tournament play, winning a gammon

with the cube still centered at 1. An undoubled gammon is worth two points.

Upside - What you gain if you take a risk and it succeeds. See also **downside**.

CARDOZA PUBLISHING CHESS BOOKS

STANDARD CHESS OPENINGS by *Eric Schiller* - The new definitive standard on opening chess play in the 20th century, this all-inclusive guide covers every important chess opening and variation ever played and currently in vogue with an exhaustive total referencing more than 1,000 openings and variations. Differing from previous opening books which rely almost exclusively on bare notation, *SCO* features substantial discussion and analysis on each opening so that you learn and understand the concepts behind them. Includes 365 completely annotated games (including a game representative of each major opening) and more than 1,000 diagrams! For modern players at any level, this is the standard reference book necessary for competitive play. *A must have for serious chess players!!!* 840 pages, $24.95

UNORTHODOX CHESS OPENINGS by *Eric Schiller* - This all-inclusive guide to every unorthodox opening used by chess players contains more than 500 weird, contentious, controversial, unconventional, arrogant and outright strange openings. From their tricky tactical surprises to their bizarre names, these openings fly in the face of tradition. You'll meet such openings as the Orangutan, Macho Grob, St. George Defense, Woozle, Elephant Gambit and even the Reagan Attack! These openings are not only an exotic way to spice up a game - but a great weapon to spring on unsuspecting and often unprepared opponents. More than 750 diagrams illustrate the essential positions characteristic of each opening. 480 pages, $22.95 (Available Fall 1997)

WORLD CHAMPION OPENINGS by *Eric Schiller* - This serious reference work covers the essential opening theory and moves of every major chess opening and variation as played by *all* the world champions. Reading as much like an encyclopedia of the must-know openings crucial to every chess player's knowledge as a powerful tool showing the insights, concepts and secrets as used by the greatest players of all time, *World Champion Openings (WCO)* covers an astounding 100 crucial openings in full conceptual detail (with 100 actual games from the champions themselves)! *A must-have book for serious chess players.* 384 pages, $16.95

WORLD CHAMPION COMBINATIONS by *Keene and Schiller* - Learn the insights, concepts and moves of the greatest combinations ever by the greatest players who ever lived. From Morphy and Alekhine, to Fischer and Kasparov, the incredible combinations and brilliant sacrifices of the 13 World Champions are collected together in the most insightful book on chess combinations yet written. Packed with fascinating strategems, 50 annotated games, and great practical advice for your own games, this is a great companion guide to *World Champion Openings*. 264 pages, $14.95 (Available Fall 1997).

BEGINNING CHESS PLAY by *Bill Robertie* - Step-by-step approach uses 113 chess diagrams to teach the basic principles of playing and winning. Covers opening, middle and end game strategies, principles of development, pawn structure, checkmate play, important openings and defenses, and how to join a chess club, play in tournaments, use the chess clock, and get rated. Two annotated games illllustrate strategic thinking for easy improvement. Includes beginner's guide to chess notation. 144 pages, $9.95

WINNING CHESS OPENINGS by *Bill Robertie* - Shows the concepts and best opening moves of more than 25 essential openings from Black's and White's perspectives: King's Gambit, Center Game, Scotch Game, Giucco Piano, Vienna Game, Bishop's Opening, Ruy Lopez, French, Caro-Kann, Sicilian, Alekhine, Pirc, Modern, Queen's Gambit, Nimzo-Indian, Queen's Indian, Dutch, King's Indian, Benoni, English, Bird's, Reti's and King's Indian Attack. Examples from 25 grandmasters and champions including Fischer and Kasparov. 144 pages, $9.95

MASTER CHECKMATE STRATEGY by *Bill Robertie* - Covers all the basic combinations, plus advanced, surprising and unconventional mates, and the most effective pieces needed to win. Players learn how to mate opponents with just a pawn advantage; how to work two rooks into an unstoppable attack; how to wield a queen advantage with deadly intent; how to coordinate movements by pieces of differing strengths into indefensible positions of their opponents; when it's best to have a knight, and when a bishop to win. 144 pages, $9.95

WINNING CHESS TACTICS by *Bill Robertie* - 14 chapters of winning tactical concepts show the complete explanations and thinking behind every tactical concept. Players learn how to win using pins, single and double forks, double attacks, skewers, discovered and double checks, multiple threat tactics - and other crushing tactics to gain an immediate edge over opponents. Learn the powerhouse tools of tactical play to become a stronger winning player. Includes beginner's guide to chess notation. 128 pages, $9.95

THE BASICS OF WINNING CHESS by Jacob Cantrell - A great first book of chess, in one easy reading, beginner's learn the moves of the pieces, the basic rules and principles of play, the standard openings, and both Algebraic and English chess notation. The basic ideas of the winning concepts and strategies of middle and end game play are shown as well. Includes example games of great champions. 64 pages, $4.95.

CARDOZA PUBLISHING BACKGAMMON BOOKS

BACKGAMMON FOR WINNERS by Bill Robertie - Newly revised! The world's best backgammon player (and two-time world champion) provides easy-to-understand expert advice on the basics of playing and winning at backgammon. 10 fast-reading chapters show the basics of setting up a board, how to move, the opening strategies and replies, middle and end game tactics, basic probabilities, plus back game and doubling strategy. Includes two sample games with move-by-move insights.160 pages, $9.95

BACKGAMMON FOR SERIOUS PLAYERS by Bill Robertie - Written by the world's greatest player over the last two decades, serious players learn all-important opening strategies and replies, middle, end and back game techniques, tournament strategies, advanced doubling cube play, and fascinating strategy moves. Also covers backgammon probabilities and odds, unusual plays, priming strategy, essential bearoff play and more. Includes example games from the masters with the thinking behind each and every move. 200 pages, $14.95

EXCELLENT CHESS BOOKS - OTHER PUBLISHERS
- OPENINGS -

HOW TO PLAY THE TORRE by Eric Schiller - One of Schiller's best-selling books, the 19 chapters on this fabulous and aggressive White opening (1. d4 Nf6; 2. Nf3 e6; 3. Bg5) will make opponents shudder and get you excited about chess all over again. Insightful analysis, completely annotated games get you ready to win! 210 pages, $17.50.

A BLACK DEFENSIVE SYSTEM WITH 1...D6 by Andrew Soltis - This Black reply - so rarely played that it doesn't even have a name - throws many opponents off their rote attack and can lead to a decisive positional advantage. Use this surprisingly strong system to give you the edge against unprepared opponents. 166 pages, $16.50.

BLACK TO PLAY CLASSICAL DEFENSES AND WIN by Eric Schiller - Shows you how to develop a complete opening repertoire as black. Emerge from any opening with a playable position, fighting for the center from the very first move. Defend against the Ruy Lopez, Italian Game, King's Gambit, King's Indian, many more. 166 pages, $16.50.

ROMANTIC KING'S GAMBIT IN GAMES & ANALYSIS by Santasiere & Smith - The most comprehensive collection of theory and games (137) on this adventurous opening is filled with annotations and "color" on the greatest King's Gambits played and the players. Makes you want to play! Very readable; packed with great concepts. 233 pages, $17.50.

WHITE TO PLAY 1.E4 AND WIN by Eric Schiller - Shows you how to develop a complete opening system as white beginning 1. e4. Learn the recommended opening lines to all the major systems as white, and how to handle any defense black throws back. Covers the Sicilian, French, Caro-Kann, Scandinavia; many more. 166 pages, $16.50.

HOW TO PLAY THE SICILIAN DEFENSE AGAINST ALL WHITE POSSIBILITIES by Andrew Soltis - Terrific book emphasizes understanding the ideas behind the Sicilian so that you'll not only play well against any sound White opening - you'll actually look forward to 1.e4! Learn to turn the Sicilian into a fighting offensive line. 184 pages, $13.95.

BIG BOOK OF BUSTS by Schiller & Watson - Learn how to defend against 70 dangerous and annoying openings which are popular in amateur chess and can lead to defeat if unprepared, but can be refuted when you know how to take opponents off their favorite lines. Greet opponents with your own surprises! Recommended. 293 pages, $22.95.
- ENDGAMES -
ESSENTIAL CHESS ENDINGS EXPLAINED VOL. 1 by Jeremy Silman - This essential and enjoyable reference tool to mates and stalemates belongs in every chess player's library. Commentary on every move plus quizzes and many diagrams insure complete understanding. All basic positions covered, plus many advanced ones. 221 pages, $16.50.

ESSENTIAL CHESS ENDINGS EXPLAINED VOL. 2 *by Ken Smith* - This book assumes you know the basics of the 1st volume and takes you all the way to Master levels. Work through moves of 275 positions and learn as you go; there are explanations of every White and Black move so you know what's happening from both sides. 298 pages, $17.50.

- MIDDLEGAME/TACTICS/WINNING CONCEPTS -

CHESS TACTICS FOR ADVANCED PLAYERS *by Yuri Averbakh* - A great tactical book; complex combinations are brilliantly simpified to basic, easy-to-understand concepts you can use to win at chess. Learn the underlying structure of piece harmony and fortify skills through numerous exercises. Very instructive, a must read. 328 pages, $17.50.

BIG BOOK OF COMBINATIONS *by Eric Schiller* - Test your tactical ability in 1,000 brilliant combinations from actual games spanning the history of chess. Includes various degrees of difficulty from the easiest to the most difficult combinations. Unlike other combination books, this one provides no hints, so you'll have to work! 266 pages, $17.95.

STRATEGY FOR ADVANCED PLAYERS *by Eric Schiller* - Recommended for intermediate to advanced players, 45 insightful and very informative lessons illustrate the strategic and positional factors you need to know in middle and endgame play. Recommended highly as a tool to learn strategic chess and become a better player. 135 pages, $14.50.

HOW TO BECOME A CANDIDATE MASTER *by Alex Dunne* -The book that makes you *think* is packed with tips and inspiration; from a wide variety of openings in 50 fully annotated games to in-depth middle and end game discussions, the goal is to take your game up to the Expert level. A perennial favorite. 252 pages, $18.95.

KASPAROV TALKING COACH™

SAITEK - The World Leader in Intelligent Electronic Games

AMAZING NEW TALKING TECHNOLOGY - Wow everyone with this incredible table top computer chess unit that not only informs and encourages you throughout the game but provides tremendous flexibility for both playing and coaching. Even more amazing, this **talking chess computer** retails for under $100!

POWERFUL AND VERSATILE - SETTINGS FOR EVERYONE - Play at any level you like - **384 level/setting combinations** and a built-in library of 134 opening moves allow a full range of options. Beginners can use the levels and features to learn, intermediate players to become stronger, and higher level players to take the challenge head on.

GREAT FOR LEARNING - Improve your chess or play for fun! The user-selectable **Talking Coach** includes learning, coach and warning modes (lets you know if a piece is in take), while the smart hint key suggests moves when you need help. If you change your mind and want to see how a game plays out differently, use the take-back feature; it allows take back up to 6 moves.

READY FOR ACTION - Sensory style chess board comes with built-in handy storage compartment for the pieces. Turn off current game at any time and continue play later - computer remembers position for up to two years.

To order, send just $99.95 for the Kasparov Talking Coach.

KASPAROV CHESS GK2100™

SAITEK - The World Leader in Intelligent Electronic Games

THE BEST VALUE MONEY CAN BUY! - The **fabulous** Kasparov GK2100 is the **most popular** chess computer we sell. Using a super high speed **RISC** computer chip and rated at a **2334** USCF rating, you'll have consistent challenges and excitement. Coaching features and fun levels makes it suitable for novices; masters and experts will want to choose higher levels.

GREAT DESIGN - Packaged in a sleek, handsome cabinet suitable for your living room. No need to find a partner to play - **take on the Champion!**

POWERFUL PROGRAM FEATURES - **64 levels of play** include sudden death, tournament, problem solving and beginner's. Shows intended move and position evaluation, take back up to 50 moves, and user selectable **book openings library**. Also choose from **Active, Passive, Tournament, complete book, no book**. Select the high speed **Selective Search** or play against the powerful **Brute Force.** program. Thinks in opponents time for best realism. Shutoff, shut on memory - remembers game for 1 year!

GREAT FOR BEGINNERS AND MASTERS ALIKE! - This **awesome program** can beat over 99% of all regular chess players, yet it is still suitable for beginners and intermediate players: Simply set the skill level to the appropriate strength for the best challenges. Matching your skill to the correct level of play ensures a **challenging** and **exciting** game.

EVEN MORE FEATURES - Opening library of 35,000 moves, **large LCD** shows full information and keeps track of playing time. Modern ergonomic design goes well in living room.

To order, send $199.95 for the <u>Kasparov Chess GK2100</u>

QUALITY BACKGAMMON SETS

Get ready to play backgammon, and improve your game. These deluxe backgammon sets come complete with Uria checkers, dice, and dice cups. Dimensions given with the case closed.

PLAYER SET

Quality velour-covered field plus smart touches of leatherette points are housed in a handsome velour exterior case with solid brass latches .

15" x 10" size - $49.95
18" x 12" size - $69.95

The Player Set

VISCOUNT

For real looks and playing pleasure, the *Viscount* comes with genuine leather exterior, suede field, and solid brass latches.

Tournament size
18 1/2" x 12 1/2" - $99.95

The Viscount

PLAY BACKGAMMON WITH THESE BEAUTIFUL SETS!

Let's Play! Enclosed is a check or money order made out to Cardoza Publishing for the desired items above. Shipping charges are listed below.

Cardoza Publishing, P.O. Box 1500, Cooper Station, New York, NY 10276
Call Toll-Free in U.S. & Canada, 1-800-577-WINS; or fax 718-743-8284

Please include $10.00 postage/handling for U.S. orders; CANADA/MEXICO double; other countries 4X. Orders outside U.S., money order payable in U. S. dollars on U. S. bank only.

Indicate desired item(s): _____   _____

NAME _____

ADDRESS _____

CITY _____ STATE _____ ZIP _____

Order Today! 30 Day Money Back Guarantee!   Back Serious

TOURNAMENT CHESS CLOCKS

Tournament Player

Tournament Pro

Saitek Game Clock

TOURNAMENT-STYLE CHESS PIECES

Tournament Staunton (Standard - Not Shown)

TOURNAMENT-STYLE CHESS BOARD

Tournament Board (Standard - Not Shown)

TOURNAMENT-SYLE CHESS EQUIPMENT
Our Recommended Chess Shop

TOURNAMENT-SYLE CHESS CLOCKS - *the finest chess clocks made*

The elite and dependable European chess clocks are fine precision made instruments **used worldwide** for tournament play and home use. Two **precision** mechanical clocks are housed together in a durable case and work as follows: The clocks are pre-set for the time limit in the game, and after one player has moved, he hits the button on his side of the clock. This button stops his clock while simultaneously starting his opponents. Likewise, when the opponent has moved, he hits his button to stop his clock and start the other one.

Great for tournament play and five minute chess! Choose from these two clocks:
1. **Tournament Player** - Hard plastic housing - $89.95
2. **Tournament Pro** - Handsome, wooden housing - $149.95

NEW! - ULTRA MODERN CHESS CLOCK - *from Saitek*

The **ultimate** in time control for chess and other board games, this clock is taking the chess world by storm. Includes **21 timing combinations** (FIDE, Club, Rapid, US Active, more!), and wide choice of settings (Tournament, Blitz, Hour Glass,, more)! Highly visible 17mm clocks.
222A. Saitek Game Clock - Ultramodern and stylish - shows time to the second! $99.95.

TOURNAMENT-SYLE CHESS PIECES - *European craftsmanship*

All our pieces are guaranteed against defects and will provide quality play for years to come. The Staunton is the classic and standard design for chess pieces. These wood fine pieces give you the feel and look of chess sets as you think they should be.
3. **Standard Staunton** - A solid basic set made of wood with king 3 1/2 inches high. Weighted and felted. $39.95.
4. **Tournament Staunton** - Hand-crafted from maple with natural and walnut finish, these handsome pieces give you the tournament feel. Heavily weighted and felted - the king is 3 1/2 inches high. Our most popular pieces. $79.95.

CHESS BOARDS - *European craftsmanship*
5. **Standard Board** - Solid design features inlaid sycomore and walnut. Good basic choice for a casual set. 1 9/16" squares. $39.95.
6. **Tournament Board** - Beautiful high-polished wooden board inlaid with maple and walnut. Finished on four sides. Four felt points on back protects tables. Two inch squares. $79.95.

PLEASE FILL MY ORDER TODAY!

Yes, I would like to order quality chess pieces, boards and/or chess clocks. Enclosed is a check or money order to:

Cardoza Publishing, P.O. Box 1500, Cooper Station, New York, NY 10276

Call Toll-Free in U.S. & Canada, 1-800-577-WINS; or fax 718-743-8284

Please include $8.00 postage and handling for the first item ordered for U.S., $3.00 for each additional item; CANADA/MEXICO double; other countries 4X. Orders outside U.S., money order payable in U.S. dollars on U. S. bank only.

Item _____ Price _____
Item _____ Price _____
Item _____ Price _____

NAME _____
ADDRESS _____
CITY _____ STATE _____ ZIP _____

30 Day Money Back Guarantee!   Back Serious

HANDHELD CHAMPION BACKGAMMON
SAITEK - The World Leader in Intelligent Electronic Games

CHALLENGE THIS GREAT <u>HAND-HELD</u> **BACKGAMMON GAME** - This pocket-sized handheld champion is fun, exciting and ready to play. **Perfect for travel** - it fits into your pocket, briefcase or sports bag and has no playing pieces to worry about. Take it anywhere you go!

GREAT GAME FEATURES - Easy to play: the LCD display **shows full game board** - no need to worry about losing pieces; directional key enters moves; computer automatically rolls the dice (or roll yourself - dice supplied); offers, accept or reject doubles; **computer remembers game** - turn on to resume play. You can even set-up your own games!

10 LEVELS OF SKILL, 3 STYLES OF PLAY - The **power and versatility** of this 32K program is amazing! Computer emulates styles of actual human players with **30 different combinations** of playing strength and aggressiveness, 10 levels of skill and 3 styles of play. Build up your confidence from beginner to tournament winner.

FEATURES, FEATURES AND MORE FEATURES! This **amazing** game has a built-in coach and tutor and can suggest best moves available . It allows take-back, rejects illegal moves and even **plays against itself**! LCD shows evaluation of position, the probability of a blot being hit, pipcount and the **complete** game statistics and score!

WANT MORE? - **4 games in one!** Play Backgammon, Jacquet, Tric Trac and Moultezim! Try to beat the computer or use the coach at the same time to improve your game!

To order, send $129.95 plus postage and handling to:

<u>Cardoza Publishing</u>, P.O. Box 1500, Cooper Station, New York, NY 10276

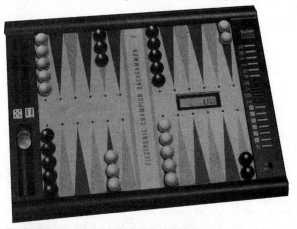

POWER BACKGAMMON STRATEGY
2 Master Books - Unbelievable Value!

Bill Robertie's Inside Winning Strategies - Now Available!

A MUST FOR SERIOUS PLAYERS!
This is the strategy package serious backgammon players must have! You'll receive these two great strategy books, Advanced Backgammon Volume 1: Positional Play and Advanced Backgammon Volume 2: Technical Play, musts for players looking to win.

LEARN FROM THE WORLD'S GREATEST PLAYER!
Go from beginner to winner! Bill Robertie's powerhouse package is designed to take you all the way. This **tremendous** course, personally written by two-time world champion Bill Robertie, is packed with **winning information** in **easy**-to-follow steps, shows you how to raise your level to competitive and even **expert club play**.

BILL ROBERTIE'S COMPLETE WINNING COURSE
For the **serious** player, the new editions of these two big volumes cover the full gamut of expert play: Learn positional play, opening, middle and back games; blitzes, priming games; technical play, endgames, races, bearoffs, and advanced checker and cube play.

LEARN HOW TO THINK AND PLAY LIKE A PRO
Each strategy is explained in words and shown in examples and sample games so you understand the concepts and reasoning behind every strategy play. Each page is jam-packed with insights, diagrams and the thinking that goes into every move. With brilliant analysis throughout, you'll be winning more than ever before and will rise to new levels!

550 SOLID PAGES/TWO MANUALS
The best advanced strategy on backgammon ever written gives you two bound books containing over 550 pages of solid winning information.

To order, send $69.95 plus postage and handling to:
Cardoza Publishing, P.O. Box 1500, Cooper Station, New York, NY 10276

Two master books for serious backgammon players